Tin Can
Treason

Terry Nardone

To my friends at Barnes & Noble Bookstores

Terry Nardone 12/17/2021

DEDICATION

To my friends and family for their love and
support.

CONTENTS

PREFACE

We were warned not to write about anything in our letters home of what happened aboard the ship, although I did keep a diary of events during my time on the ship and the story herein is a full recollection of my combat tour of Vietnam.

Many military people and various Veterans have told me, that I may have been one of the youngest, lowest ranked Sailors ever officially nominated for the Distinguished Service Ribbon, not to be confused with the Distinguished Service Cross. The criteria of the nomination indicated that the nominee must have exhibited outstanding service above and beyond what would be normally expected in their official position. This would be regardless of rank or MOS (Military Operational Specialty)

I have placed into words here all I could reflect upon, including what we the crew learned, and what we were informed of concerning events which took place aboard the ship that could be considered treason.

Should you read this memoir, maybe you will agree with the Engineering Officer, who nominated me for the ribbon. I only know one thing for sure - "I did the best that I could".

Over the years since my discharge from the Navy I was vigorously involved with the VVA (Vietnam Veterans of America). A fellow VVA member knew of my involvement in an attempted memoir of my combat tour. He gave me copies of excerpts from a book concerning the type of operations he was involved in during the war, he felt these excerpts were pertinent to my story of being on a destroyer in Vietnam. A paragraph from the book 'Infantry in Vietnam' is quoted below.

Use the available tools

Naval gunfire support has also proven to be a valuable adjunct to the operations conducted by the free world forces in South Vietnam. In all of the corps areas it is possible to engage many enemy targets with naval gunfire from ships at sea, and it has become the rule rather than the exception for US, South Vietnamese and their allies to plan for and employ this fire when operating near the coast. With the help of naval gunfire, two ARVN popular force platoons not only defended their outpost at My Trang, they were able at the same time to inflict grave damage on a reinforced enemy battalion bent on the destruction of their position.

From the Book: Garland, Albert N. Infantry in Vietnam. New York: Jove, 1986. Print.

Beyond my involvement with veterans, I have sought the advice and words of wisdom from various authors on publishing my memoirs. The following review was sent to me via the internet by Robert K. Wilcox, an author who had read a first draft of my book.

"Terry Nardone has written an unknown story about his time in the Vietnam War serving on a destroyer. It's about the 'little Guy' who must fight the war at the whim of those making decisions. I only saw the first draft of this book, but the story has elements of 'The Caine Mutiny', 'Mr. Roberts' and 'Catch 22' – all of which eventually became movies. If Terry's final draft fulfills its promise we may all be seeing his story on the silver screen." - Robert K. Wilcox, author of Black Aces High, Wings of Fury and Scream of Eagles.

Illustration 1: Graduation From Hull Maintenance Technician's School, San Diego 1972

Text 1: Terry Nardone Fourth Row, Third from Left

ACKNOWLEDGMENTS

Photo Front Cover

USS Bordelon (DD881)

Photo by

PHCS W.A. Jackman
No: USN 1106742

Book Cover

Design by Michelle Nardone

Mango Moon Studio

Inside Photos

Taken by Terry Nardone while
in the service.

1 ENLISTMENT

It is sometime in the late 1970's after my discharge from the Navy and I am sitting in a space, which I jokingly refer to as my orifice, instead of my office, an opening into a world previously unknown to me. My work is done at a folding table, c-clamped to the wall for sturdiness. There is no heat duct in the room. I sit on a "super hot seat" left over from a Buffalo Bills football game. There is an Agent Orange poster on the wall. My insides sour thinking of the others who have been exposed to it. In the middle of the Pacific Ocean, I was ordered to dispose of fifty-gallon drums and was written up for refusing to do the detail without some type of protective clothing. I still do not have any hair where the oozing yellow liquid spilled onto my legs.

The photo is there on the wall along with the others. The one of that tiny American Flag in front of the giant behemoth black memorial where it all started for me. It was the first time I had ever done anything with another group of veterans. Together we took a trip to the dedication of the Vietnam Veterans Memorial in Washington, D.C. There is also a group picture of the men I served with aboard that dull gray ship. The twenty-eight-year-old creaking beast, which cracked from the vibrations of firing her own guns. Twenty-eight is old for a ship and she was a destroyer commissioned in 1945 just in time for WWII to end and she never saw any action in that conflict.

Papers upon papers are everywhere. Responses from Congressmen and prospective employers. Newsletters, pamphlets, schedules, and meeting minutes, along with phone numbers and names dealing with

Vietnam Veterans and others. I started working with the Vietnam Veterans of America, Chapter 20 from Rochester, New York. My duties include being the Assistant Chairman of the Legislative Committee and I am working diligently at my designated tasks.

I have been in counseling for about six months and have been told I suffer from one of the worst cases of post-traumatic stress disorder the Veterans Outreach Center has on their roster of client's. The counselor believes I have had a nervous breakdown and the only course of action is to apply for public assistance, commonly called welfare and my whole family is dependent on it for the time being.

I kept a dairy of my daily life aboard the ship from a tour of Vietnam and decided to write about my experiences. I am not an author, so I will do my best to retell my story. The military creed comes to mind, *I will utilize any and all available resources to the utmost of my abilities in order to gain the goals of my unit whatever those shall be.* Here my journey begins.

When the Gulf of Tonkin incident hits the news, I am still building B-17 bomber models and trying to get up the nerve to ask a girl to the freshman dance. I am cutting out news articles from Vietnam and keeping a scrapbook, but it all scares me to the bone. The draft is what scares me the most, hearing about it in school and having nightmares that my number will come up and I will die in the war. My family could not understand why it upset me when my cousin was born. I had learned about a draft rule called, sole surviving son, before my cousin was born. I was not eligible to be drafted, being the sole surviving son in the Nardone family.

I have recurring thoughts of going to war. Go! Go! Go! The draft haunts me. I am registered at the local community college, and decide to blow the fifty-dollar registration fee and go to the Navy recruiter. I enlist as soon as possible, when I turn eighteen, because I do not need parental permission. I call my father from the recruiter's office.

"Hey dad, I have a physical exam tomorrow in Buffalo."

He is silent.

"Why do you need to go to Buffalo for a physical exam, we have a family doctor, you know."

"I joined the Navy and the exams all take place there."

"You never told me you were thinking about enlisting, we never discussed it." He replies.

"and you never asked me about the divorce from my mother either, so I guess we are even now, anyway if I pass the physical, I am in and I will get a guaranteed school after boot camp, according to the recruiter."

"I don't know what to say to you, my only son."

"I guess all you can do is wish me the best of luck." I said.

"You are right."

Click!

The adrenaline is flowing, and my nerves are acting up already. I have never been this excited or confused ever in my eighteen years on the face of this planet. I joined the Navy, because I did not want to go to Nam and that was that.

Two weeks later, I awake in a barracks with various other men. I am pulled from the line of guys who went in together from Buffalo, and I am put into a holding company. What the hell is a holding company anyway? Needing to know, I ask one of the officers in the barracks building.

"Well, you see this company has all types of men that have had some type of problem."

"What type of problems?" I ask.

"Well, we have a guy from Kentucky, who has never worn shoes before and he needs special attention for that problem."

"In your case, you did not pass the eye exam and need glasses." He responds.

"Are there any guys in this company from Buffalo that have joined the Navy instead of going to jail?" I ask.

"Yes, there are." He answers.

"As a matter of fact, we have several who were convicted of assault with a deadly weapon and they are all in this company with you."

"You are supposed to be a squad leader and have done a pretty good job so far. The racial tension is awful and you handle it well." He said.

Racial tensions are high at the time, I would learn months later all about it. The Navy had a recruitment effort to encourage men to enlist by sending minority recruiters to inner city neighborhoods to give speeches about the benefits of signing up, and is useful in upping the minority enlistment from ten percent to over thirty percent.

"We usually have a group of men from the same recruiting station, but here we have inner city, all the way to no shoes from Kentucky. You should have a good time in the Navy, you are made for this type of life."

"I am afraid for my life is what I am, based on the felonious members of this company."

"This conversation is over, Seaman Nardone. I have work to do and you have your new duties, this is not the Boy Scouts, this is the Navy! You had better be ready for anything to happen. The racial tensions are, Bad! Bad! Bad! I do not want to talk about it any longer. The last holding company in here, six men went to the brig and one got a BCD."

"What the hell is a BCD?" I ask.

"Those initials stand for a Bad Conduct Discharge. The recruit ended up going back to the judge in his hometown and on to jail. You just watch out and keep up the good job that you are doing."

"That is not proper English sir and you should know that."

"Get out of here you wise ass! Your main problem is you are too smart for your own good and it shows, the other guys do not like it. Now get out and go back to your duty station, wherever that was when you were called to talk to me."

I leave and return to the barracks.

My country has always been a source of pride for me and I loved it greatly. What was I going to do now that I found out about the men I was serving with? I go through many changes during boot camp, just as I am sure others do when they enlist, overnight a grown-up bad ass and all of that crap. Put on a uniform and you can get cocky fast. Some guys volunteer for Nam and really want to go bad. Two guys went to Seal School and I was off to do technical training in what is commonly called, "A" school, where I will train to keep the ship intact. I learn about fighting fires and controlling battle damage, praying I would never have to use my newly acquired skills.

When graduation from "A" school is near, I fill out a dream sheet, which involves picking three places where you would like to be stationed and what type of ship you would like to be aboard. I want to travel and like a fool, I remember the recruiter's words, *if you like the idea of travel ask for a Destroyer*, and this is what I did. I ask to be stationed at Charleston, South Carolina, because I had met a girl who lived there. I got what I wanted a Destroyer home ported in Charleston, South Carolina.

2 ABOARD THE USS BORDELON

USS Bordelon (DD881), she has millions of miles on her and an eerie feeling of past crew members, like an old hotel that has been renting rooms for decades. Many men have slept in my PIT, a nickname for your bunk or RACK. A three-decker canvas roped to an aluminum frame, and hanging by chains. I go on a whirlwind tour of both coasts to attend school, first Philadelphia and then San Diego, before reporting aboard. I had never been on a ship before. My rate as Shipfitter and Damage Controlman has been combined to the new rate of Hull Technician (HT) and we learn everything about keeping the ship secure as well as maintained. I did better in HT school, than even I thought was possible and graduate near the top of my class. During training they show films of the fires aboard the USS Forrestal and my dreams change from being drafted and dying of bullets to burning up alive. I realize my rate and my actions might save lives (especially my own), even if we are not sent to war. It is instant dedication to duty.

The conveyor belt in constant motion spits luggage from its rubber-toothed mouth. People mill around and wait for their baggage to appear. It is hard to tell your duffel bag from the next one. I pick one up and have a rude altercation with the owner of the duffel bag, who points out his name on the side.

On the flight to the East Coast, I show pictures of my graduation from Hull Technician School to the stews and they comment about how many pictures they have seen from men in every branch of the service - "We could write a book of all the stories." Travel is what I   liked about the military in the first place and here I am at my final resting stop, Charleston, South Carolina. Mingling around are other short hairs and everyone is asking the question whether they are going to the Air Force Base or the Navy Base. I catch a cab with some Navy Base riders. "Where are you from?" If I had a buck for every time, I have been asked this question since my enlistment, I would have a bundle of bucks. The ride is short and the base seems surrealistic, like a giant bubble.

The cabbie coughs at the gate guard.

"Here is a load of boots ready for the high seas."

"How do you know they are all boots?"

"I asked them all."

Replies the cabbie.

The gate guard bellows,

"I will need your orders and ID cards, all of you."

"All of you get out and I will examine your stuff one at a time."

We all exit the cab and the cabbie lights up a cigarette as he waits, which he has done a hundred times before. I gaze into the distance as we meander. The scene before me looks like a nighttime football game, only during the daytime. Huge lights everywhere, intertwined with the ship's mast lights. I hand over my stuff and await a reply. No reply, only a return of the paperwork and ID.

"Everybody back into the cab. They all go to pier Delta and should be able to find their way from there."

The guard exclaims.

We reenter the cab and await the trip to board our ships for the first time. The piers look like a landing strip for UFO'S. Phone booths and poles are the only things resembling a city. The cab drops me at the gangway of DD881 and asks for the fare. This is it! The first time aboard a ship after sixteen months of training. I stomped up the aluminum gangway loudly never having used one before. *Hand to fore head salute*, I militarily mouth.

"HT3 Nardone reporting as ordered sir."

It is a Saturday and the whole place is deserted. The watch officer gives me the once over as I drop my duffel bag with a thump. He writes something in the watch book as he reviews my orders and here it comes again.

"Where are you from, HT3 Nardone?"

"Rochester, New York." I respond.

"Oh yeah, the camera place. That is all I know about it."

The officer yawns.

"I will have your duty division person come and get you. You will not meet everybody until Monday, since it is a Saturday and then the work starts."

They pass the word over the PA system, which I learn is called the 1MC (1 Main Circuit) for the duty R-Division to report to the gangway. Repair division is a part of the engineering department and is made up of Machinist Mates (MM), Hull Technicians (HT), and Electrician Mates (EM).

I am introduced to a Petty Officer Second Class Machinist Mate named Dennis Mengel, who takes me to see my new quarters. I will stay here for the next thirty-six months with twenty-five other guys in a space the size of a small living room.

Mengel is jovial and says.

"I'll wait till later to find out where you are from and get you introduced to the other duty person, who can get you situated, he is also an HT (Hull Technician). Follow me and be careful with your duffel bag, it is a steep drop down these ladders."

I slip and hit my head anyway, even with being extra careful. We go to find the other HT. His name is Mike Sanchez and he is from Texas. Sanchez tells me there is only one locker and two bunks open, so I can have my pick.

I respond.

"I do not have much of a choice, do I?"

He told me to use the lock off of my duffel bag to secure my locker after putting everything inside. Sanchez sits down and talks to me about all types of things. He is really surprised when I tell him that I can speak Spanish having learned it in high school and also from listening to tourist training records.

Sanchez asks.

"Did you go to school before getting to Charleston?"

"Yeah, both in Philly and San Diego." I respond.

"How long have you been in, Sanchez?"

"Two years." He replies.

"Do you want a cup of coffee while you figure out your locker?"

Sanchez and I will eventually become very close. I will frequently go to his house for dinner and chatter. Out of all of my friendships, our friendship becomes one of my closest. I learn after about six months, that there are relationships like this all over the ship.

When Sanchez returns, I comment to him.

"This locker sure is small!"

"It is only three by three by one and it is all you have got. You learn to cram stuff in and keep it organized."

"Where is everybody, Sanchez?"

"They live off the ship and they are only aboard for duty when they have it."

"It will be nice, to stay in one place for a while, after traveling to different places" I reply.

Sanchez laughs.

"*Scuttlebutt* has it that we are leaving in ten days for somewhere. Nobody knows where."

"What is *scuttlebutt*? They didn't use that word in boot camp?"

"BOY YOU SURE ARE A BOOT ARE'NT YOU!"

"*Scuttlebutt* is the nickname of the ship's gossip. Don't worry you will get used to things in a hurry, that is the way it seems to be."

Sanchez explains.

"There are two other new guys in the HT shop, who have come aboard in the last two months. Neither one of them have been on a ship before. You may get your sea legs pretty soon!"

"We do a lot of reading around here, what type of books do you like?"

"Science Fiction." I reply.

"Mengel loves Sci-Fi, he will have some good ones for you to read."

He pointed to a small light at the top of the rack and tells me the best place to read a book is in your bunk where nobody will bother you.

"Well Nardone, let's go find Mengel and he can show you around, I need to get some rest for the mid-watch."

Sanchez exclaims.

Mengel wants to go to the mess decks to watch a movie that they show every night. I meet a few guys while I am unloading my bag and trying to fit the stuff into my locker. I only have four dungaree uniforms, two dress uniforms and a few civvies (civilian clothes). There are a couple of plastic boxes for the small stuff and that was it. I also have my used Zeiss Icon camera with me left over from a high school photography class. I would rearrange and move things in my locker a hundred times or so, just for something to do over the many months to come.

"Okay Nardone, let's go to the mess decks and I will show you everything later. There will be an official tour tomorrow to break you in." Mengel comments.

We use the one passageway down the center of the ship. It seems like walking in a storm drain to me. Everything is gray or white and the lights are bright making everything seem harsh and hard.

"Well it is all made out of metal, you fool, it should look hard!"

Mengel laughs.

There is a sheet hung in the middle of the mess decks and you are able to watch the movie from either side. Mengel introduces me to everyone. There is a wide variety of shapes and sizes, but always the same question, "Where are you from and what is your rate?"

I don't remember the movie only the surroundings, the scene before me is like a movie itself. Dungaree clad men lounging everywhere and smoke curls in the projector's beam, then Mengel tells me, "You should see it when we are out to sea and half the crew wants to watch a flick."

Mengel shows me around after the movie, and we play at introductory conversation. He takes me down to Bravo 3 through hatches in the deck which lead to the boiler rooms below.

Mengel relates.

"This is where I stand watches when we are underway and I have what they call the four and eights, four hours of watch and eight hours off, just like the watches they had you stand in boot camp only on a different schedule."

"We just dropped an electrical board during testing and all kinds of work is going on. The R-division (repair division) works hard all the time as something is always breaking down. In the machine shop we   have a lathe to make spare parts when we have to instead of ordering them. *Scuttlebutt* around the ship is that we are preparing to go to Nam."

My eyelids popped!

"You're nuts! This ship is on the east coast. I volunteered for this coast so I would not have to go to Nam."

"Well, Nardone, lots of ships have gone to Vietnam from this east coast of ours. We are also supposed to go to New York City for the Fourth of July, but there is a shortage of personnel."

It is so loud in the hole it is like sitting under the hood of a car is how I would describe it.

"Nardone, my guess is that the trip to New York City is in preps for going to the war and that is one long trip. Let's talk about something else. I am a pacifist hippie and I only enlisted for the free education and a little adventure."

"What kind of books do you like?"

Mengel inquires.

"I like science fiction."

I reply.

"We swap books with each other which we have already read, by writing our names in the cover and waiting for our names to come up, then you can give it to the next name on the list."

We go to his locker and talk some more about everything.

"Time to hit the pit, Nardone, see you in the morning.

Welcome aboard!"

We both laugh.

I wander around and feel out my new home, as I will be here for the next three years. There are pelicans on the pier and millions of stars above. Everything is harsh and hard on the ship, surrounded by soft sounds on the brightly lit pier. Not having separated myself from it fully, I decide to call home from a phone booth on the pier. It is two in the morning and my father will be asleep on the couch with the television on. What the hell, I needed it! My father and stepmother thought I was goofy anyway.

Afterward, I felt worse and decide to try out my pit. There are no blankets, then I remember Sanchez explaining to me earlier, if I used one belonging to someone else who was not aboard, but at home, there would be trouble. Rules! Rules! Rules! The military world is completely different from the civilian world. Without a blanket, I am freezing while sleeping in the air conditioning. A rough night, Hell! I have to get up in four hours anyway.

The whistle blew my brains out at 0700 and the day started off all wrong when I catch my foot in the bunk chain and fall roughly to the deck. Scrambling to my feet wearing my spiffy new dungarees makes me feel out of place. Some guy nicknamed Bobo (Richard James), whom I met the night before brought some guys over to meet the new "boot". I also meet my shop supervisor, Petty Officer First Class, Leroy Sass. He is one of the smallest men I have ever seen. All in all, everybody is jovial and friendly, but some guys look like birds of prey waiting to jump on a piece of food. Leroy gives me my own coffee cup and a roll of toilet paper.

Leroy is laughing loudly as he tells me.

"Sometimes we run out of this stuff up in the head and last week I sold a roll to a guy for five bucks. I get a kick out of catching them with their pants down, Nardone, and just remember to take a roll with you, checking first to see if there is any in the head. I can always sell you a roll, you know!"

Sanchez seems eager to befriend me and asks me to go to the chow line with him. We walk down the port side and I salute an officer, who was traveling in the opposite direction. Sanchez did not salute. The officer asks me to come and see him in his quarters after chow time was over at 1330. I think I am in trouble and Sanchez tells me to not worry at all. The galley is on the port side, all the way forward. At breakfast everyone fills up on eggs and sausages.

Illustration 2: Petty Officer First Class Leroy Sass (Left) Petty Officer Third Class Michael Sanchez (Right)

Sanchez informs me there is a shortage of men in the Boiler's Mate Division which will cause us a problem with the trip to New York City, along with the entire operation and the preps for the trip to Nam.

"You really think we are going to go don't you, Sanchez?"

"I know we are Nardone and that is that. I have connections in the right places and I have been told the Captain is mad as hell, because they will not transfer a boiler tech in time to make it for, exercises we are to participate in, as part of the trip to New York City."

Sanchez yawns and said he has not been sleeping well aboard and tells me.

"If we do not participate in the operations, we probably will not go to the war zone and the Captain will not be pleased."

"Hey, Sanchez, I am not certified for the watch that you stand, you know Sounding and Security, but I could fill the place of the boiler tech and stand watch in the hole, so the ship can make the trip to New York City."

"Well, why don't you volunteer and see what the Captain and the Engineering officer have to say about it. You just may get us into the war zone and make the Captain very happy. He is a warmonger and really wants to go bad, my contacts tell me."

We finish chow and I go to the officer's quarters, as Sanchez instructed me to do earlier. The officer informs me that we are all, *Tin Can Sailors,* and we do not salute officers as on other ships. Everybody knew this was the way it worked. He asked me to please get used to being on a destroyer and not do it again. As I leave the officer's quarters, he asks the same question.

"Where are you from Nardone?"

"I am from Rochester, New York, you know the place where they make the cameras and the film."

"Yes, I know all about Rochester in Upstate New York. I went to school in Newark, New York."

"Nardone, you can leave now and just remember this is the 'Tin Can Navy', and it is different from anything else."

Back in the HT shop, I talk to Leroy and the Engineering Officer about standing watch in the hole.

"You really want to go to war when we have a good chance of not going. The Captain will love you if it works out and you can stand the watches."

The deal worked and two days later the announcement is made at quarters for muster and inspection.

The Chief announces.

"Men - in two days we will be leaving for the 1972 Fourth of July celebration in New York City. The real purpose of our trip will be Operation Agate Punch, which we will be a part of off the coast of North Carolina. We will be doing operations with the Marines. This will be a ground forces support and landing exercise."

Mengel ribbed me and said, "It sure sounds like we are prepping in North Carolina for North Vietnam." *Scuttlebutt* flew everywhere. How the hell did Sanchez know?

After quarters all the Hull Technicians meet in the shop to get ready for the day. I am being introduced to the ship's Planned Maintenance System work requests and my fellow hull techs. We will also have fire and flooding drills during Operation Agate Punch. Here we go, more drills just like school, Drill! Drill! Drill!

Leroy informs me of my duties. I will concentrate on Damage Control and work requests, but leave the welding to the more experienced. I am told to work with another HT, Sebastian Riccobono, a tall bespectacled guy from Milwaukee, Wisconsin. Bobo warns me he is a hard ass and so while I work with him there will be no fucking up or around. We are assigned to PMS (planned maintenance systems). The day goes well and I am introduced to lots of guys with the same questioning stance "Where are you from? Where are you from?" Sometimes I wonder if there are men on the ship whom I have never met and I come to the realization the expression, *Tin Can Tight*, basically means you know everybody and many bonds are made over time.

The ship will leave soon and I am asked to go over (the navy term for crossing the gangway and going out). We are going ashore to the "Flying Dutchman", the biggest bar I have ever seen. It is built inside of a WWII bomber plane hangar. It is now a public place and does not house planes anymore. On the stage, the rock group 'Commander Cody and the Lost Planet Airman' is preforming. The music is good and as usual I drink too much. I am reminded of the reason I requested to be stationed in Charleston, the drinking age was eighteen.

During Operation Agate Punch, I stand a watch in Bravo 3 and keep an eye on a coolant gauge and make sure it stays at one hundred and ten degrees, while chatting with a new found friend, Victor Pajaro from Columbia, South America. He had joined a special program that allowed him to transfer from the Colombian Navy and become a U.S. citizen along with all of his family, even his cousins. The military will do just about anything to fill the ranks, as I had learned in boot camp.

I practice speaking Spanish with Victor and we became very close friends. We stand the *mids,*(watch rotation from 1200-1600 midday and 2400-0400 midnight) together and it is always one hundred degrees in the hole and a huge vent fan blows air into the space. Everybody talks two tones above normal and you have to shout if you are more than ten feet away. We drill and drill and go to General Quarters at all hours. My GQ station is the amidships gear locker. It is full of all types of equipment needed for pumping water and fighting fires. I am in charge due to my training and my Hull Tech's rating.

3 OPERATION AGATE PUNCH

The ship takes on a life of her own, like some gray behemoth from down below. I have a feeling like we are in the lungs and she is alive. Why do we call her she anyway? The men seem to be the bloodstream flowing and giving her life. You became a part of her, feeling like she was alive, because of you, and could not survive without you.

She couldn't live, could she? I love the ship and the sea. The sea taunts me. I wallow in every moment of it and cannot believe how much I enjoy it. One night on watch, Pajaro's instincts arose and he beckons me over to him.

"Listen Nardone, Listen to that noise."

The rumbling, hissing, and clanking noise all flows into a deafening noise for me. "Over there Nardone!" Over there!"

He points and motions me to follow. We move slowly and I await the loud BOO! of a prank. We stop and he changes direction, deciding to go up the ladder.

"No, no, it is down here, follow me."

We go down to the bilges and he lifts up the metal plank of the floor.

"There it is that little monster over there!"

He points to a valve and takes a wrench from his bag of tools, to adjust a nut on the valve. It is all Greek to me and Pajaro makes me listen and put my ear right next to the valve assembly as he adjusts the nut. I could vaguely hear the difference in the hissing noise coming from the valve. He checks a gauge and determines everything is okay now.

"This is the way you get after fourteen years down here. I have been in the hole since I was a Fireman, and now I am a Petty Officer First Class. I have been down in the hold after we drop the load and there are no lights, it is really scary."

I pray I will never see it happen. I am in awe of what had just happened and did not speak for the rest of the watch, except for some Spanish practice with Pajaro. I also help Pajaro with his English, which is maybe at a sixth-grade level.

We all have to work eight hours and stand eight hours of watch. Leroy's gift of a coffee cup sure comes in handy. I am given the detail of making the morning coffee replacing Riccobono. I am told it is tradition to have the most recent crew member take over the coffee detail. The coffee pot being an old percolator, it took forever to make a pot.

The operations off the coast of North Carolina last two weeks and we have three days in New York City. We pull into the harbor under full dress as they call it and have flags flying from the fantail to the fo'c'sle wire atop the main mast in a "V" shape. The ship looks impressive. There is a huge crowd watching us pull into the Port of New York and it all seems surrealistic to me.

During Operation Agate Punch setting condition three is necessary, meaning all exterior hatches have to be secured and no one is allowed to open them, only if we change emergency conditions. I awake one morning to find my wallet missing. We secure our pants to the bunk chain with a belt and I was foolish enough to leave my wallet in my

22

pants pocket. I went nuts.

"Who the hell stole my wallet! Who the hell did this to me?"

I rant.

Leroy comes up to me and asks what is going on and I tell him my wallet had been taken from my pocket while I was asleep. I am hysterical, ranting, and raving about the pictures in it and my ID card.

Leroy with his fifteen years of experience in the service and time aboard ships knew better. He took me over to the trash can and there was the wallet. I am about to grab it, when Leroy grabs my hand and tells me to leave it alone. He leaves me there to watch over the trash can, while he goes to tell the Master-at-Arms, who will contact NIS (Naval Investigative Service) and they will do a full-blown investigation. NIS shows up via motor whaleboat and boards the ship using the rope ladder. They remove the wallet with rubber gloves, take my statement, and place the wallet into a plastic bag. They take fingerprints from the wallet and determine whose they are. The perpetrator is taken to the brig on the Marine base. He is a Boatswain's Mate. The whole incident really changes my idea about who your friends are. Sanchez gets mad as hell, when I think it might be a member of the repair division who had taken it.

There are two types of men aboard, lifers and short-timers. There are big differences between the two. The eight-hour watches, and working is taking a toll on me and I learn the mid-watches are the worst to stand. Hell, they are all a bitch to deal with.

When we come back to Charleston, I am invited over to Sanchez's house for dinner and meet his wife and kid. I also befriend Bobo, Riccobono and Jack Kelly. We discover there is cheap beer at the Air Force Base. We drive to the beach, drink the beer and build sandcastles. Are we men or boys?

After a month of fun, the *scuttlebutt* comes true. The idea hovers in the back of everyone's mind and is always a part of the conversation. Neuman and I discuss the war. He is a pacifist hippie type that was in for the free education and other benefits. I visit him on duty while he stands his watch, and we talk about war in general and what it is all about.

The silent reaction at quarters smells of fear. Wives and families are to be left behind, many men live right here in Charleston with their families, just like Sanchez. Not a hit and miss around the map like some groundpounders (ground-based units of infantry soldiers), all at once we are on our way to Nam. The chief is having difficulty finding his words and did his dutiful best. He maintains his military monotone but hurt shows in his eyes.

"Men there has been a lot of *scuttlebutt* going around about all the hard work and the Yardbirds (civilian workers). Well there will be a lot more work. We are preparing for a lengthy cruise and it is called WestPac. I have been there before, but for those of you who do not know, it means we are going to the Western Pacific and doing a tour in the war zone called, Vietnam."

He drones on.

"This info is not for public knowledge and only immediate families are to be told. We all know there is a war going on and now we are part of it. The orders have been signed and that is that."

He looked scared as he approached the end of the statement then as quick as he started, he just stopped talking and everybody is dismissed. He had forgotten to ask if there were any questions and there were many, too many to remember. One guy asked how long it would take to get there. We were informed the cruise would last forty-eight days. Forty-eight days to get to the war in this old beast. Later in the day a man said how important R-Division is to the soundness of the ship.

We are finally dismissed and later in the shop Leroy told us more *scuttlebutt*.

"The chief believes the Captain volunteered us to make the cruise and that is that. My guess is the *scuttlebutt* is true, knowing he is a warmonger and war is the quickest way to advance in rank."

I spend the rest of the day ranting and raving about volunteering for the east coast so I would not go to Nam and here we were going. What the hell! I was being a spoiled brat, not thinking about the other guys and it showed. There are many comments made about how much sex will be going on and everybody laughs. Sanchez is very disturbed about leaving his wife, who is pregnant. Wives visit every night when their partners have duty and I witness many crying as I walk around the ship. I am busy partying all the time and do not know what else to do but party.

Talk about the war is at the center of every conversation lately. I am at Sanchez's house for dinner again and see how far along his wife is. The baby might possibly be born before we get into the war zone. The weather in Charleston has been hot as hell and the home-cooked meal at the picnic table tastes great. Sanchez and I had similar backgrounds as kids and would continue to get close.

At dinner I am thinking about what Jack Kelly told me about Sanchez's wife being loose as a goose and screwing around anytime Sanchez was on the ship for duty. Jack also tells me wives seem to be this way, and he wonders how a marriage could survive the military, telling me the divorce rate is twice that of the civilian population. Sanchez wants to be a lifer and is extra dedicated.

The conversation turns to talk of destroyers and how they are a *loose* ship without many starchy rules and regulations. Talk aboard other ships was that you could spot a *Tin Can Sailor* by how ragged his dungarees were. Sanchez informs me the expression, *Tin Can Tight,* is a banner that some guys have sewn on their civvies to show pride, meaning the ship was small, we were all cramped together and we all knew each other. We talk of our dedication to duty and I tell him I am definitely dedicated to my rate.

Mike comments that we especially had to take good care of the head because the Navy sometimes scares the shit out of every Sailor. We all laugh.

Some asshole put the entire crew on extra watches by an act of sabotage. The announcement is made at quarters for muster and inspection the next day.

The Chief makes the news sound good and bad, like he wishes it would happen, so early in the morning standing in line and listening about what was going to happen for the day.

"Men an inspection of the main turbines has turned up a well-placed wrench. If we had tested props with the wrench placed where it was, there would be extensive damage. Now, don't get me wrong it was a twenty-five pounder and it would have created havoc. Someone obviously does not want to go to Nam and I do not blame them."

He became more serious and orderly.

"There will be a cold-iron watch (when a ship stops operating its own plant and is receiving services from shore) in all the holes from now on and you can thank whoever placed the wrench there. So, if any of you know who it is you should turn them in. The watch will be four and eight just like when we are underway the only difference being, there will be more men to stand the watches, but you will all have to stay. I repeat that many men are going to be separated from their wives and families because of this incident and if anyone knows who did this, they can be assured that no one will ever know who turned them in."

Bob Neuman has cold iron watch on my duty section and I visit him and talk about his hometown of Boston and how long the war has been going on. Bob had been in college and was a war protester before being in the Navy. He had lost his draft deferment, because he could no longer afford to attend college.

"What the hell are we doing here, Nardone? We will never win this war, only destroy the whole dammed country with Napalm and Agent Orange. I do not believe in this war and look at me now, I am going to be part of it and have no choice but to be dedicated to my duties because of friends like you."

Neuman is livid.

"All we do is kill, maim, and take body counts. Shit, there has been more fighting in that little country than in WWII and we do not even have fronts or anything. I have studied this war. Do you know we were backing the French in 1958?"

"Shit, Neuman I was only five years old." I said.

"Well, I was older and had problems from the start. If you follow the news, the war may be over before we get there, Paris peace talks are taking place every day."

There is a long pause as neither one of us speak.

"We have known each other for a while now, Nardone, and I have got to tell someone, because you will not tell anyone at all and I trust you."

"Tell someone what, Bob?"

"Here we are alone in Main Control together and I am going to tell you - I am the one who put the wrench in the works."

"I do not believe you, Neuman! I do not believe you! You are just telling me that, so maybe I will turn you in and get the reward. You didn't do it and I don't think you feel like doing time in the brig."

Someone must have had the same idea as Neuman, because the perpetrator confessed after a friend turned him in and he is sent to the brig. Is that better than going to war?

Little incidents like this keep cropping up as I read my diary and type the words to tell my story. *I will use any and all available resources to the best of my ability in order to reach the goals of my unit whatever those shall be.* Is that correct or is it a little different. Everything is done to the best of my recollection and I cannot remember everything or maybe some things just do not seem important.

4 LEAVING FOR THE WAR ZONE

Time is getting short and we will be leaving with the flow of the tide in seventy-two hours. The fear is still evident among some of the crew. I have become friends with the Quartermaster and he shows me the map of the world and the charted course we will be taking barring any unforeseen circumstances.

I also befriend Arroyo. a friend of Pajaro's. He works in ECM (Electronic Counter Measures). He explains to me all about his rate and what his duties are. Both Arroyo and I go to visit and chat with the Quartermaster. We ask him how many miles the trip will be. He tells us it will be about twenty thousand nautical miles round trip which sure sounded like one hell of a lot of mileage to travel. He outlined the area known as the "Devil's Triangle". There is a book being passed around the ship about this area of ocean and it wore out before I had a chance to read it. The whole book just fell apart. What a hell of an omen to go through this area on the first part of our journey. The turbulent war years, so much is written about them now. We are all a part of this history and will probably be studied in books someday. Going through the Triangle will come to be much less traumatic than the departure.

On the pier it looks like a college campus protest. I am busy and only come amidships at the last minute, just as the lines are cast off and the crew takes their places. Wives and children are yelling, screaming, waving, and blowing kisses. Just like a scene from a movie. My feelings zip me in half. I do not know if I want to go or not. I sure as hell wish I had someone to blow kisses at me, but I didn't. The departure is made worse by the protesters on the pier. They have their permits and have the signs up - "STOP THE WAR! DON'T SEND ANY MORE TROOPS TO BE KILLED! STOP THE WAR!"

Many people have traveled from far away to say farewell and here is everybody on the pier protesting, what a send-off. Admirals and other officers are in attendance. My rage is matched by many of the other men and their families. We thought there would be riots. I wonder how many times before this scene had played out.

Friendships between families who knew each other are torn apart by differing opinions. My anger does not subside for days. I rant to anyone who will listen, "What a send-off!" On our way to war and possible death and here we have to face this. The television crews using us for their own views.

Sanchez's wife is there with her placard of protest, she did not believe in the war. What a conversation must have gone on in his house. Sanchez the lifer and the war protester wife.

Lots of guys, especially from the rural areas want to go and cream the commies and are always talking about the war and winning it. What a diverse crew. There are so many viewpoints, war, no war, why war? What the hell, it is pandemonium.

We have to travel quite a distance down the Cooper River before we will be ocean-bound. The old Charleston area scenery is gorgeous and we lick at it like little kids with lollipops. Many of the chiefs have seen this before and I am in the hole when we start out for Operation Agate Punch. A casual acquaintance points out to everybody that his family lives on the edge of the river and they have a big sign held up with the words, "Good Luck!" Only minutes from the sea, the triangle and now the war is only days away.

A seventeen-year-old from Dundee, New York arrives via helicopter when we are in the Devil's Triangle. He is a blond virgin and we try to get him laid in Panama but he isn't having any part of it, saying he is saving himself for a future bride that he has yet to find. On the trip through Panama, there is lots of partying in the EM (enlisted men's) club. There are the whores, the drugs and the booze. There are no prescription laws in Panama and you could buy anything you want. All types of guys buy amphetamines and barbs. They are buying everything.

A Kentucky Fried Chicken in Panama! I have a long conversation with Mengel about how we are fighting in the Vietnam conflict, so McDonald's and Kentucky Fried Chicken can open up in Vietnam. What great international relations that would be. Dennis has studied Communism and said that it is just one step better than a dictatorship, you could not stop it, because much of the world is so different than the United States. Going through the canal takes eight to twelve hours. We prayed we would go through in the opposite direction.

The day before we go through the Panama Canal, we do not have to work too much, due to high seas of fifteen degrees port and twenty degrees starboard. It is a really rough trip and to tell you the truth, I am scared!

A new guy is transferred aboard, who will take over the watches in Bravo 3 from me, since I have been qualified to stand "sounding and security" watches now. On watch I spend my time roving the ship, checking every compartment on the hour for fire or flooding. Using a metal tape measure with a weight on the end, I lower it into the hole to check the water level in the voids. A void being a place that has no entrance other than the hole to take the measurements. I also check the ASROC (Anti-Submarine Rocket) decks for security purposes and am told to shoot anyone trying to enter, even the Captain, unless there are orders to enter. The entire crew knows the ASROC's are capable of nuclear warheads, but none of us ever knew if they were armed with them or not.

I am standing a lot of mid-watches and drinking plenty of coffee, maybe about fifteen cups a day and the Doc warns me about too much caffeine. I try to cut down, but just keep getting a cup every place I visit on watch and it ends up being a spree of sorts. As we travel through the Panama Canal, men are watching the Baseball World Series on Spanish television.

The HT's participate in flushing out the salt water from the water system as we pass through the fresh water lake section of the canal. A water fight breaks out, shoving each other around with the water from the hoses. Another division is caught up in the fun and after a half an hour the Captain calls a halt to it, telling us to act our age. Act our age, I am only eighteen years old! The chief requests a swim party while we are at anchor in the lake. He is denied because of the threat of sharks and we all know they could not survive the fresh water. Do they have fresh water sharks?

We are at sea five days just to get to the Panama Canal. Most of the men on the ship go to the same club at liberty before we enter the canal and it is a typical Seafarers nightclub. We raise hell, sing songs and listen to live music. Many people are on the streets at 0200, and as I remember from my days in school, this is the Spanish lifestyle. On October twenty-first as we pull into Roma, the ship we are relieving from the gunline in Vietnam is coming in the opposite direction. Men are waving at us from the ship and it seems like a scene from a WWII movie.

On the Pacific side of the canal we party some more. Are we men or boys? There is a lovely young girl in Panama that wrenches out a piece of my heart forever. She is a prostitute and I am reminded of the movie, "Ship of Fools." The heat is frightful in Panama. The Jungle is so dense you can only see twenty feet before everything is a blur. We meet Marines training for their tour in Nam and they tell us what the jungle training is like. We are then warned of fights between Marines and Sailors which break out at the club in Panama. Vietnam lurks in the not too distant future.

We have Pacific Port Quarters for muster and inspection as we are leaving the canal.

The officer speaks.

"Men we are just beginning our journey. Many men going through the canal for the first time. I am sure it was an adventure for all of you and now we are headed for another adventure. This is one of the longest distances a Destroyer travels without hitting a port of call. The solitude and the sea will daze us all at times. You might come down with cabin fever. There will be a chess tournament to help pass the time. Try to stay loose, keep busy and talk a lot to pass the time and calm your nerves."

Illustration 3: Leaving the Panama Canal

He continues with regular Quarters instructions especially about haircuts.

"I want everyone making regular trips to the barber shop. Hair length will be checked before anyone leaves the ship in Hawaii at the gangway, and if it is judged to be too long your liberty will be canceled."

It has been raining all morning and at 1245 we pull out for Hawaii. It will be necessary to refuel at sea and this is something we practiced and prepared for during Operation Agate Punch.

I am enrolled in the chess tournament where I get my ass kicked by the "R" division Ensign. There is news on the radio and Panamanian TV that a cease-fire in Vietnam may come about on November twenty-fifth. Everyone is talking about it and the *scuttlebutt* travels quickly. We have a daily General Quarters drill which is timed by the Quartermaster from start to finish and we feel like we are running races.

I am on the highline (the line from ship to ship to hold the fuel hose) detail during refueling and replenishment. Just like the days of old, we heave and ho and pull the line over from the other mother ship, as Bobo calls it. Here we are on the way to war, when back home the World Series is on, reminding me again of WWII. Even with a war and all, they are still playing baseball back in the United States.

As time drags on, we are getting very intimate in our conversations. The talk goes far beyond the usual, where are you from, to talk of wives, beliefs, families, hunting, hobbies and everything you can imagine. Instilling deep trust between us, such as between Neuman and I during the wrench episode. Later in coastal waters, Sanchez and I talk about how we have trust in each other, more than he has for his own wife. He then admits to me, he does not even know if the baby is his own and how loose his wife is. He must really be in love.

It sure has been a long growth period for me in only a period of eighteen months, feeling as though I have aged years, not too many months out of high school. As thoughts of death surround us, we become more and more intimate and reflective with each other. I have developed a brotherly love for Sanchez and Pajaro, then I wonder where my trustworthy answers will come from for their questions.

Leroy has been acting funny while we are out to sea and we suspect that he has a stash of beer somewhere aboard. We start the Leroy vigil to see if we can catch him in a drunken position. Of course, you could hardly tell, because he always has a drunken appearance. After three days, Leroy takes Bobo on a tour of the ship only to have a stink bomb dropped on his head.

Are we men or boys?

The Captain has just announced at quarters that even if there is a cease-fire, we will not have our tour shortened. There will be lots of fighting still going on, as everyone will not adhere to the peace treaty. On October twenty-fourth I make a comment in my diary that I am thinking about home and my ex-girlfriend. These are the kind of thoughts that keep you going.

What we wouldn't give for a snack! Leroy had a party in the shop and we found out he has stowed three jars of peanut butter and five boxes of crackers he bought at the PX (Post Exchange) in Panama. Every night we have mid-rats (midnight rations), mostly bologna. It sure tastes good and we eat heartily. Eventually they have to limit mid-rats for only the men standing a watch, because so many are coming to eat. What else was there to do at midnight?

About five days out of Panama, MM2 Barber runs into me on the fantail and he thinks I look depressed.

I said, "Who doesn't?"

We both laugh.

He knew I was relatively new aboard and there is something he wants to show me. We go way up to the fo'c'sle railing at the peak of the bow on the main deck. Looking straight down from here the ship slants backwards. We lean over the railing, the wind blowing like crazy and in the ocean playing by the wake of the ship are a half-dozen dolphins. The sonar is loud up here and Barber tells me the dolphins have been following us since leaving Panama. A feeling of being kids revealing a secret hiding place comes over me, so beautiful to watch and being a Walt Disney type, I love it up there. The dolphins jump over the wake from side to side chasing the front of the ship. They would speed up and jump across the bow. Barber said they eat the garbage we throw off the fantail and might follow the ship all the way to Hawaii. Making their noises and playing hard, like nothing I have ever seen before.

It is the escape of all escapes and I will bring Sanchez up there to see it later. Sanchez is amazed, not ever having seen dolphins before. The wind, wake and dolphins are wonderful. Even with this escape you still could not stop thinking about the war and what we might do in the action. I wonder if there will be a name for any of the operations, we might participate in.

On October twenty-seventh about a dozen of us take showers in the rain. The fresh water consumption is always a topic of quarters and we have a rotating watch to make sure the men only use the water for fifteen seconds to water up and fifteen seconds to rinse off. We grab asses in the rain, the shower feels good, and I soap up like crazy.

The blues are starting to set in. We have been away for almost two weeks and Kelly tells me we have downshifted from our normal routine and have become accustomed to the trip. The jokes are less frequent and there is a droop to everyone.

I get my sea legs on Agate Punch and am very happy, because the water is rough lately. As fate would have it, on the roughest day of all, we must refuel at sea. Refueling and the *helo* (helicopter) detail are the most dangerous things we do, other than being in the war zone. My detail is on the highlines, as we maneuver alongside another ship, an oil tanker, the other mother ship as she is fondly called. The ships must maintain the same speed and stay parallel. I get ready to pull the refueling hose over to our ship. There is a cable that is very tight connecting the two vessels. The hose is on pulleys attached to this cable and we try to line it up for a perfect hit into the female receptacle aboard.

With the ships close together we create a channel and the seas are extra high. We have been getting soaked since coming alongside the other mother ship. Manny Terrazi and I are at the end of the line. A big wave washes up, we get soaked and the force knocks Manny all the way down the side of the ship. I see the life-jacketed body getting washed along the deck. He just misses getting thrown over the side of the ship and is all tangled up in the guard cables. He is all bruised up and the Doc gives him three days of bed rest. Many guys stop to see him to find out what it was like. He is a very popular guy with all of the crew.

I am playing cards a lot and watching every movie when I am not on security watch. My back is giving me problems and hurting. I complain to the Doc and he says I will have an x-ray in the Pearl Harbor Hospital. I can't sleep especially after the highline detail. I keep thinking if I had been on the end of the line it may have been me who almost went over the side. More GQ drills and more neatness means liberty. There have been a few guys denied liberty because of improper dress. We are not allowed to wear our uniforms on shore due to an executive order, because of the problems with the way people treat the uniformed person. We will be pulling into one of the largest and most infamous Naval places in the whole world, Pearl Harbor!

On November first we are about eight hundred and fifty miles from Pearl Harbor as the drills continue. Drill! Drill! Drill! We are learning about our new positions as US Naval Gunfire Support which we just call NGFS. We do not secure the ship in the same way as when we have general quarters, we have to set all the hatches to condition "Zebra" which is on a certain amount and type of hatch. We all have special stations and mine is in the forward gun mount loading projectiles into the gun mount. Later I would change to setting fuses in the aft gun mount.

I am very depressed today, making note of it in my diary. We have not received any mail since Panama and will not receive any even in Pearl Harbor, because of some snafu where our mail was sent to an oil tanker and never transferred to the ship. I am lonely even surrounded by a hundred men.

I am waiting in the chow line and talking to EM Mike Davis as he complains,

"You know we are in a prison, don't you? The ship is a dull gray and white, we are all dressed up in our dungarees and we are unable to go anywhere. They muster and inspect us every day and tell us what will happen with our lives. The only difference between a prison and the ship, is that there are no bars on the windows and we must obey the rules."

"It's the sacrifice we have committed to for our country, Davis." I respond.

"Then why do I feel like I have committed some crime, Nardone? Many times, I think of this ship as a prison."

"Gee, Davis, you are so cheery! We are not depressed enough and you have to bring up prison. I hate to say it, but you are right, it is like a floating prison at sea."

"Someday Nardone, if we make it through all of this you will have to come down to Louisiana and I can take you out fishing on the bayou."

"Someday you can come to Upstate New York, Davis, and we can go ice fishing. Have you ever been in the cold weather?"

"No never, I have never even seen snow, Nardone, I was in boot camp in the middle of the summer."

"Let's get our food and sit together for a change of pace."

"Sounds good to me! We can chat more about this ship being a floating prison."

Friendships are getting tighter as time goes by and I am getting close to so many men. I cannot keep track of all the times I think about all of us dying in the war and never seeing each other again. Many men have this feeling and are sharing their innermost thoughts with each other. There is a club like atmosphere on the fantail. We use it as a meeting place where you can get fresh air and relax, as if it was possible! We sit atop the lowered flag mast and tell jokes about the largest drag racer on the water. Destroyers being the fastest oceangoing vessel.

There are favorite gathering spots all over the ship. Some spots are better than others, like atop the rear gun-mount on the fantail. We named it the rear penthouse and would ask anyone we did not want there to leave us alone. It was like a club in a tree house.

Are we men or boys?

A favorite gathering place is anywhere with a good pot of coffee. We drink coffee all day and all night. I drink it as if it were the nectar of the gods. Keeping me awake and great to have when you were down. We carry our coffee cups attached to our belts by filing down the handle and using a key chain clamp to secure it to your ass.

We sunbathe on the rear flight deck and find out getting a sunburn is considered destruction of government property and punishable by Captains Mast. We do crazy boy things to pass the time, and we have not made Hawaii yet. At the rear penthouse atop the gun-mount I would daydream about Horatio Hornblower books I have read. What crazy gutsy men they must have been to sail in those wooden ships. Rough seas aboard this ship were enough for me. Imagine those crazy bastards pulling up alongside each other and blowing the hell out of each other with old-time cannons. Reading about the naval war in the Pacific against the Japanese in WWII, the book took on a surrealistic meaning to me and I thought about Pearl Harbor a lot.

Every inch on the Quartermaster's map brings us closer to the war. Every night on watch I have to report to the bridge once every hour and write in a special log. Talking to the engineering officer, who is also on watch I ask him to show me the specs for a destroyer. I read in awe about the destroyer's specifications.

A destroyer is three hundred ninety-eight feet long and forty feet wide, the smallest and fastest ocean-going Navy vessel, built for speed and maneuverability. The hull is thin and not built to withstand enemy attack, but is a vessel for escorting larger vessels in a fleet and to defend them against other attackers. No wonder they called it, *Tin Can Tight*! We are packed into a small space doing our time and doing our jobs.

I laugh and ask the Engineering Officer.

"So, we are expected to outrun the bombing of the Vietnamese?"

He did not laugh, replying this is basically the truth and we would do zigzag patterns in the ocean to avoid getting hit by any shore batteries.

We continue to talk about Pearl Harbor and how good it will be to get some liberty, feeling the war creeping closer with every port of call, next Midway Island and then on to Guam. As we get close to Hawaii, we pick up satellite television. Watching the news, there it is, more about the peace treaty, the war, body counts and the bombing raids, nothing has changed in ten years. There is talk of a big push by the United States to end the war.

Are we being sent as part of the big push? I visit one of my friends in the ship's office, where the Personnelman works, who had all the info on everybody. The Personnelman receives some *scuttlebutt* from the home office in Charleston. The rumor is a bunch of misfits are being transferred to the Bordelon, because we are going to Nam. He relates some crap about how some men are being transferred directly from the Marines stockade and the brig. Obviously, these men have the choice of the war or the brig as a punishment. Other guys are sent to our ship from Captains Mast on other ships and obviously are given the same choice, brig or war. What a crew! A bunch of misfits and criminals, just what you need for shipmates.

Hawaii is now only thirty-five hours away and I cannot wait. The tide is supposed to be just right for pulling in at the thirty-five-hour mark, which makes everyone happy. We finally arrive only to wait and wait and wait! There are problems, nobody knows what they are, but waiting sure causes grumbling as we sit and look at Hawaii from miles away and wait some more. The Executive Officer makes an announcement on the 1 MC. The snafu is straightened out and in fifteen minutes we will be going in. Everyone assumes their temporary stations as the officer sets the sea and anchor detail for pulling into port.

The XO (Executive Officer) also announces.

"Men we are going to pass right by the USS Arizona Memorial and conditions are great for taking pictures. I advise you get your cameras."

The whole side of the ship is lined with men viewing the scenery. Hawaii sure is beautiful. As we come closer, WWII looms larger than life. I mean there is certainly something different for a group of Navy men, ready for war, passing by one of the most infamous spots in naval history. Everybody chats, emotions are visible on the men's faces as we view the memorial. I am scared by it all, with a feeling deeper than fear mixing with joy at seeing something few people will ever get to see and knowing that it holds more meaning for us than anyone could ever know.

The memorial is full of Sailors who died at a young age no older than we are now. The water is sparkling clean and fish can be seen swimming playfully. Tourists are wandering around.

I begin to rant and rave.

"The Sailors aboard this ship could be down there, only in the water off the coast of Vietnam!"

Thinking no one wants to listen, I shut my mouth and so do many other guys. Other men just keep working on sea and anchor detail. The Silence aboard is strange, as men turn away when approached by anybody, not wanting to think about anything. Men in the holes are relieved in order to see the Memorial and they begin to talk about being buried in a boiler room and having your soul float around forever.

A feeling surrounds me as if entering an old empty house and a bile taste comes into my mouth. The pier looms in the distance and I think about walking the ground where all those brave souls ran around against all odds and fought the Japanese. The servicemen in the past must have been in the midst of a frenzy of war and death. Will it be that way for us and what did our tour hold for us? Would we face the same things as those men faced during the attack or something completely different? Every time I went in the hole from then on, I felt like I did when we passed by the Memorial. There is nothing scarier than thinking of being trapped in a ship as it sinks. The Arizona went down in only thirty feet of water.

Mail is delivered via chopper from another ship on our way to Hawaii. After two weeks of not receiving any letters, the Post Office will be a busy place. A cherished moment in life aboard is when the letters arrive at your bunk. I also have a special stash of mail in my locker stored in a shoebox for safe keeping. When Mail Call arrives, most letters contain mundane stuff about home, the weather and the snow clinging to the trees. I am ripped between the hot and cold worlds as I read about the snow and freezing temperatures. I am thinking the snow must be pretty, but then become mad as hell as I sweat my ass off working in the hole and other hot places aboard the ship. I never write letters home about the fear, the war or any other bad feelings. My letters home, consist of news mostly about the chess tournament and my newly found friends. I also write about the experience of going through the Panama Canal and all that crap. All the letters sounded like we were living in some type of play land. I just could not tell everyone at home the truth about it all.

We shed our woes on each other and fill our bellies with booze, which only makes matters worse, as everyone is afraid. Sharing our thoughts only provides momentary relief, like Maalox for an ulcer. We did smoke a lot of dope to escape the real world. Just like taking "Maalox" for an ulcer, it only provides temporary relief. Some guys are high all the time doing a doobie before breakfast. We smoke out on the fantail and if you did not smoke dope, you dare not tell anyone what was going on for fear of being fed to the sharks and being thrown over the side.

At night all of us gather in the Electricians shop and remove one of the dogs from the entry hatch so no one could enter the compartment. We lock ourselves in and keep everything inside, both in the compartment and in our brains.

When I was alone, I would get high and re-read those letters from the pubescent plebs from home. My god! They are airheads and you could tell from the letters they sent. I would feel lonely once in a while, even being around the entire crew, I do not know why?

We pass something that makes me sick, somewhere along our journey after the Panama Canal, a garbage floe, you know like an ice floe. We guess it is three by five miles in size and there are squirrels, rats, and seagulls obviously living on it. It is garbage which has been dumped into the ocean and with currents being just right, the garbage has formed its own little island. I even think I can see plants growing on it. I hate pollution and love nature. Using the mounted binoculars on the bridge, I get a better look and it is not a pretty sight. When we dump the garbage from the ship off the fantail it provokes my anger. The mess cook puts it into perspective for me when he mentions how big the ocean is and how big the garbage floe is comparatively.

Reading my diary now, ten years later, from the WESTPAC cruise, all the expected comments are there. I miss home-cooked meals, I'm so tired, but I cannot sleep, Sanchez misses his wife and talks about her all the time and promises me a good home-cooked meal if we make it through the war. The food is good, as good as can be expected, and the mess cooks are doing a fantastic job. Some guys are getting quick tempered and snapping at other Sailors. These are all comments from my daily diary. These thoughts keep you going.

About three hours after pulling into Pearl Harbor, still in the throes of emotion from the Arizona Memorial, a new Sailor comes aboard, who will be in our division. He was flown in from the east coast and is tired. I have duty and find myself on the other side of the conversation I had months ago. Where are you from? He introduces himself as Walter Yacus and we hit it off extremely well when we find out we are both from the same area in Upstate New York. Everyone always asks, where are you from?

Illustration 4: Third Class Petty Officer Walter Yacus - Electrician's Mate

I devour every minute of meeting a newbie and show him around just as I had been shown around on my arrival. It is time for chow and we go to the mess decks. I discover we have been to the same places in the Southern Tier of New York bringing us even closer immediately. I get him situated after chow with a locker, a blanket and a rack. I have to stand watch after chow and wish him good luck and go about my duties.

About ten of us went over the next night to a bar called the Lemon Tree Lounge, who the hell picks these places! We partied like crazy at the bar and did shots of Tequila. The hangover makes things worse and I wonder if I will ever stop drinking. Five of us get together and rent a car, driving all over the island. We happen to see the filming of an episode of "Hawaii Five-O". All of us feel very touristy.

We pull out of Hawaii under another sea and anchor detail. Everybody talks about their liberty, where they went and what they did. Midway Island is one week by sea. We take on an air conditioner in Hawaii for the mess decks and spend all day on a Sunday putting it in. Since it is a wall-mounted unit, we have to cut a hole in the ship and get permission first. We would not have to sweat our asses off at chow anymore and the crew will consider the HT's heroes.

My watch cycle changes and I only have sounding and security watch every thirty-two hours. The rest of the crew is pissed at this, because they all had the four's and eight's which could really drag you out. Four hours on duty and eight hours off duty, plus you also had to work when not on watch.

Leroy and I have become the best of friends over time. He being black and me being white, he tells me he has never met anyone with less of a prejudicial attitude than me. I tell him my father has done business with many black people and he taught me to respect everyone regardless of their color or country.

A guy nicknamed Grandpa enters my mind for some reason, I write about him in my diary. We call him that because he looks so old, but is only in his thirties and looks as if he is in his early fifties. He is a lifer and making the Navy a career. He is a Petty Officer, Second Class after a stint of fifteen years and is always getting Captains Mast, going AWOL and all kinds of stuff. Everybody likes him and he tells some wild stories about his exploits and what he has been through in his fifteen years.

More General Quarters and more GQ drills. We get the timing down to about three minutes and thirty seconds to set the entire GQ detail and be at our appointed places after all the drills. We have to follow a special routine - secure certain hatches and run the pumps. Drill! Drill! Drill! We will be crossing time lines, turning the clocks back and I comment how we need to keep the time properly down to the second. We also will cross the International Date Line in a few days and then change the dates in our logbooks.

I make an entry in my diary on November the seventh, that it is a dull day. I did not laugh or feel good all day. We pull in at Midway Island and leave after only four hours, just enough time to load provisions and take on fuel. Some of the crew fish off the fantail and it is really a tropical paradise looking place. We talk about how there was a famous Naval battle here during WWII also.

My diary skips from the ninth of November to the eleventh as we cross the dateline. We get a half day off on Saturday and all day off on Sunday. We are told there have been complications with the mess decks air conditioner. On Sunday, Sanchez and I go to the rear penthouse to chat and watch the ocean pass by. We are telling each other our deepest thoughts and having a real serious conversation. The topic of Homosexuality comes up somehow and Sanchez tells me there are several guys having "affairs". I could not believe it, but he said he knew and that is that. I never suspected, being as naive as I was, things like this are going on. The Navy, of course, does not condone this type of behavior and if these men are caught, they will receive a dishonorable discharge. After our conversation we play cards. We kept winning and winning and winning and my ass gets sore from sitting on a hard tin can, which was commonly used as a seat. The more we win, the more we like it and so on and so forth.

My recommendation for Petty Officer Third Class is pulled by the lifer bastard Chief Petty Officer who is with "R" Division. He has some crazy reasons for it. I tell him most guys receive the rating right out of Navy school. He tells me you have to sign up for extra years to advance and asks me why I don't sign up for some extra time. I laugh and tell him I think we are all going to die in Vietnam anyway. Everyone thinks he is a coward and more afraid than the rest of the crew. On the fourteenth of November we receive our schedule of events which will often change, you can never have a schedule and everything is day to day, if not minute to minute. Never knowing what the hell is going to happen.

No mail since Hawaii and I long for some, just like everyone else. Some guys never get any and I feel sorry for them. There is nothing like a letter in the mail to make life more tolerable. I get a letter in Midway when the mail arrives. It is from my girlfriend Linda telling me she is so confused about my enlistment in the Navy. She does not know what to do, so she gives me a hug by mail and breaks up with me, explaining we will both be better off. This is the only letter I ever receive from her.

I am starting to be afraid now. We are getting closer to the Philippines and from there it will be the war zone. I still have told no one how scared I am and put up a macho front. My rating, being in charge of a detail in a damage control gear locker ramps up my fear. I am well-trained and knew what could happen aboard a ship even if the ship was not in a war zone. The films of the fires aboard the USS Forestall still haunts me. I believe being an only child and not having any brothers and sisters had something to do with my fear. I do not know why, but I just felt this way.

48

I create grief for myself by submitting a request to see the Executive Officer, who is commonly called the XO, to review my recommendation to become a Petty Officer Third Class. I tell him the chief seems to have a personal thing against me and did not like Italians. He is prejudice and against anybody who is not a WASP. I also inform the XO, I think the chief may be having problems making decisions, because of problems he is having back home with his wife. The chief had learned his wife wants to leave him from a letter he received in the mail. What a hell of a thing to get in the mail. You could not even consider it as a *Dear John* letter because they were married. I guess a Dear John is a Dear John no matter how you look at it. Great news on the way to the war zone! She could have at least waited to see if he dies in the war before asking for a divorce. The XO is not interested in my request and I am dismissed.

5 SUBIC BAY

On the eighteenth of November we are at sea and anchor detail as we pull into Subic Bay in the Philippines. According to our schedule this is the last stop and then it is off to the war zone. We are all old salts now considering the sea miles we have traveled and the training at General Quarters drills. Many close friendships are formed and the same guys hang around together all the time. We are told at quarters that we will be given liberty and all can go over.

The XO comes to the fantail for a lecture about where we were and what to expect. He starts his speech.

"Men this is one of the scummiest and most heavily used ports in the entire world. I am not telling you it is bad, because it is terrible!"

He drones on.

"There are fifty to sixty thousand prostitutes and two-hundred hotels and bars. The VD rate is second only to South America and the strains are resistant to penicillin. The Doc has free condoms for anyone that wants them, and are Navy issue for just this type of situation. There is also a tremendous problem with lice and crabs, and we do not want them on the ship. It would be wise to stay at a good hotel and there are a several Be aware there is Martial Law here and Americans have been killed. We lose an average of three Sailors a week who are never heard from again after going over. I must also warn you - they will not think twice about shooting you, if you are on the streets after the midnight curfew. As they say, *dead men tell no tales*! This is the way it is here!

Many beautiful handmade goods of different types can be bought here and I highly recommend that your shopping goes beyond trying to choose a whore."

He pauses and looks sternly at everyone.

"Are there any questions? Have a good time, men! This is the last stop before the gunline. You are all dismissed."

Everyone meanders about and looks for some good civvies to wear. The first stop is the Enlisted Men's Club, which was on the Navy base and held about six-hundred people. There are hookers here and many beg us to be their escort for getting on and off the Navy Base. We have been warned they will steal anything that is not attached to something else, like soap and toilet paper. There are slot machines at the EM club and I love them. I cannot wait to get my hands on them. Dump in your money pull the lever and watch the wheels spin. I would hit many a jackpot and buy drinks for everybody. Drinks at the club are served cafeteria style, you go down the line, order what you want and pay at the end. Drinks are twenty-five cents each. We all drink like crazy and smoke some great dope. I mean they had the best climate in the world for growing it and it was only five dollars an ounce.

I go with a girl named Sally to see the movie Rio Conchos. It is in English with subtitles in their language. Sally speaks some English and tells me she is a college student at a school in Manila. I have enjoyed my time with her. She shows me around and makes sure the jeepney driver does not rip me off with a high fare.

She tells me many college kids come to Subic Bay for the clubs, the music and the Sailors. I really like chatting with her and she speaks some English. There are so many clubs and whores who never stop partying.

Is it good or bad for us? I will never know. Sally finally explains to me the real reason college people come to Subic, they hope to find a Sailor to marry, in order to become an American citizen. What a world! Even offering you a good dope connection if you marry them and you could become a drug trafficker.

On my first trip out as we call it, which reminded me of the ship being a prison of sorts, a bunch of young kids stop a few of us, put the heads of little ducklings in their mouths and beg for money. If you do not pay up, they will bite the head off and spit it at you. If you pay up, sometimes they bite the head off anyway, spit it at you and say, "No balls Sailor! You got no balls!" They were all skinny and mean looking. Making you mad as hell when they did their stuff.

As soon as you exit through the main gates to the base you pass by Shit River, there is open sewage and people living on the edge of it, even in summer. Who the hell knew they had a hot season, which is their summer.

A bunch of us have our pictures taken by guys with Polaroid's, just as many Sailors have done in the past before us. There is a Marine contingent here and they have their own bars they go to. We are told not to go to the same bars, because of the threat of fights breaking out. The whole thing reminds me of the Wild West and what it must have been like.

Outside of Manila is where all the good action is supposed to be, all the money and the cheap handmade and imported goods. Some of us grab a bus ride there, which is too wicked to describe. The Filipinos are probably very happy about the war, because they are eligible to join the Navy and become U.S. citizens. The military traffic and the war are good business for everybody on these islands.

I stay at the same hooker's house most of the time and she lives on the edge of town surrounded by jungle. They say the atmosphere is as close to Nam as you can get, and I feel the war more than ever now. Soon we will leave for the gun line. We will not be in country, but I can feel what the groundpounders must feel like when they go on patrol. There are giant cockroaches everywhere and rats climb over your chest as you lie in bed. I thought I had guts just to stay overnight and leave every morning for duty on the ship. She has Paul Butterfield records and a beautiful stereo another Sailor must have bought for her.

Roaches, rats, and filth are everywhere while the stereo blasts the song, "Born in Chicago", as we smoke cigar sized joints of that cheap dope. A lizard crawls out of my boot one morning, climbs up my leg and starts to lick my face with its tongue. I was definitely scared to death.

This hooker got mad at me for some reason and chases me from the bar one night. She is throwing bottles at me and yelling something in Tagalo (her language). It was all so much fun, how can you not go crazy. On November twenty-fifth we leave for the gun line and I write about planes taking off from the airbase. I claim I can feel the war for the first time, probably because of those planes. We take on a lot of ammo in Subic and are leaving fully loaded. I am sleeping in a bunk over the rear magazine which is where they pass up the shells via a pulley type of mechanism.

6 WAR ZONE IN VIETNAM

We leave port in the Philippines and steam toward the gun line. The trip is not very long, I do not remember how long it took but it sure seems short. We start Condition III and are playing search and destroy now. We steam up and down the coast waiting for hostile fire and return fire to the position where the hostility comes from. We are sitting ducks as we steam up and down the coast. The enemy can move after shelling us for a few minutes and we have to wait to return fire until we are ready.

I am setting fuses in the aft gun mount and Yacus is handing them up to the mount crew via an opening in the gun mount. The sound I hear is a terrible, *Beep! Beep!* Warning, then *boom!* The mount goes off every time we fire. We are not at GQ but condition III and if need be can go to GQ really fast. The pressure changes as the shells leave the barrel is wicked and it hurts my ears. I want earplugs and wish they were available. We use cotton to stuff into our ears. We receive our tentative schedule and it calls for a whole month on the line doing the wait for hostile fire routine, also supporting land troops asking for incoming fire to a certain position. Schedules change though and we hope we do not stay for the whole month. We probably will be on the line until Christmas.

A line from the song, "Born in Chicago", goes through my mind - *He went down before he was twenty-one*, as my thoughts turn to a shell hitting the aft magazine and we all go down with the ship. During NGFS (Naval Gunfire Support), Yacus and I change jobs in the aft gun mount and try to keep up a good pace. Yacus takes off the nose cone on the shell and I set the fuses with a spanner wrench to the specifications they call for.

I set the fuse to PD (for point detonation) and it will go off when it hits the ground. I also set the fuse to a number to delay the explosion so the shell will go off after that many seconds in the air. Our first time on the line is the day before Thanksgiving. I have the 0400-0800 mount rotation and I realize this is no game. We are killing people with these shells that I am setting the fuses on. Spreading death and destruction all over the place.

George, a Gunner's Mate, takes me to see the fire control bubble in back of the bridge on Thanksgiving Day. We are on holiday routine and George thought I might like to see where they control the shooting from. He sat inside of a half-rounded Plexiglas shell with foot and hand controls. He sits in the bubble and it rotates in the same way as the gun mounts. It is like pointing a gun and pulling the trigger. He claims we are so accurate that we can hit a truck six miles away with the proper coordinates.

I am amazed and think about what it must be like for George up there, seeing all the action and firing the Big Pistol as he refers to it. Days are long on NGFS, starting my mount watch at 0345 finishing at 0715, then working all day and back on watch until 2000. The guns were still going off, making it hard to sleep and then word comes over the 1MC (public address system).

"All hands stand clear of the main decks while taking hostile fire."

All the hatches are secure and we are able to go to full GQ in less than three minutes. The ship is shaking and rattling most of the time and the pressure changes are terrible. We have a full power run to head off some NVA that were crossing the DMZ and this made the old beast feel like she was going to disintegrate. The sounding and security watches are always watching for a seam to burst or a line to break. Guys go all over the ship to try to find a quiet place to sleep and Yacus is able to sleep right in his rack. I will never figure out how he did this. I try climbing into all the bags of laundry outside of the laundry. I burrow in like a mole and still cannot fall asleep. The bags were big about fifty pounds apiece and I find someone else in there one night trying to sleep. There is no escape from the *Beep! Beep! Boom!*

Yacus and I joke to pass the time. We can hear the guns going off on the beach or close to it. We hear a *Ping! Ping!* noise all the time and wonder what it is. I call the bridge and ask what the noise is. The response makes me crazy with fear. Yacus asks what the hell is wrong and I tell him the response from the bridge.

"The noise we hear is shells exploding really close to the ship, sort of like a ricochet or something."

I continue.

"It cannot be true Yacus, the sound is happening about every fifteen seconds and that is only the close ones. Butch (Yacus' nickname) get me the first *helo* out of here. I cannot take this war zone crap anymore!"

"Hey Nardone, what are you worried about, it is only a sound, and if a shell hits in the right spot we will never know what happened anyway. The sharks will have their dinner spiced and diced."

"No one will ever know anything about us if we take a hit in the right place and who cares there is no escape from any of this and we just have to live with it, Nardone."

"You are right, Butch. If we are not loading and setting fuses, they have a better chance of hitting us. Besides we are doing zigzag patterns in the water anyway, can't you feel the ship moving that way?"

We have to change the watches around, now I am on the 1200-1800 and 2400-0600. They ran out of Willie Peter (white phosphorous illumination rounds) up in the forward magazine and we must form a line all the way from one magazine to the other and pass the shells hand to hand. Leroy gets us some rest afterward. I only had two hours until watch anyway.

The chow tastes great, because right now it is the only recreation aboard. I am losing track of days and feel lost. Why not lose track of time, we are all locked up and the guns have been going off for about seventy-two hours. A special detail has been set to cool down the gun barrels with extended nozzles on the end of a fire hose. The guys tell me that it hisses like hell when the water hits the barrel and they have to stand back from the spitting of the hot water.

On the twenty-ninth of November I go nuts. I start beating on the shell with a spanner wrench and yelling at Yacus. I was hoping it would blow up and kill me. Yacus talks some sense into me and I settle down.

We look for a downed pilot for about three hours late in the day but only a few men are allowed outside with binoculars. While we are searching, the gyro compass stops working leaving us dead in the water, as they say in the Navy. What a feeling! The ship is unable to move. We are looking for the pilot and are far from shore, Thank God! We would have really been sitting ducks.

Leroy comes to us with the *scuttlebutt*, we have sustained damage from firing the guns and will have to return to Subic Bay for repairs. This ship is old and she just cannot take the guns going off all the time. Leroy always seems to know everything.

So, I ask.

"Hey Leroy, what if we take a hit and we can be sent back forever?"

"Nardone, all the Chiefs have the *scuttlebutt* going around that the Captain volunteered us for these war games."

"That is just wonderful, Leroy, the whole crew already hates that lifer's guts and now there is this crap to contend with."

The 1MC crackles with the official news.

"Men we have sustained some superficial damage and are departing the gun line to return to Subic Bay for repairs. We have received a word of thanks from the Marines for our last stint of NGFS. They say we did one hell of a job and got them out of a jam. Thank You!"

Realizing everyone must work together, even if you are killing people with those shells that you set the fuses on, I am haunted by the fact that one mission is good and receives thanks and another mission goes bad when you hear screaming over the headphones and are told the shells are hitting the Marine's position and killing our own troops.

Some of us overcome our prejudice just by realizing that the man next to you, no matter what color or ethnic status he may be is the one that may save your ass and by this, I mean your life. Sanchez has a talk with me lasting from one watch to the next. We talk about his being a Mexican and the fact that he is having a rough time making Petty Officer Second Class. He feels the chiefs are against him because he is Mexican and they will never change. He asks me if I ever thought of his ethnic status and I told him only when I look at you. We both laugh.

For the most part I was hurting inside all the time and was having a problem with such deep relationships. I was an only child without a brother or sister and here I am befriending Mexicans and learning to speak Spanish better than ever before. I obtain the nickname *Gringrito*. A few weeks later I find out the translation is little white boy!

I am scared and confide in Sanchez, wondering why nobody else seems to be. He said everybody is scared to some degree and just have different ways of dealing with it. He is angry with me for smoking dope all the time and tells me some day it will come back to haunt me. I still wonder if I would have nightmares and problems if I did not get stoned. I was still young and all I knew was doing it made me feel better and took the edge off. I also was drinking to excess.

While we talk, we touch each other, a hand on a shoulder or a punch in the belly. It is the first physical contact I have known with a friend. This is a new experience for me. How can any of us combatants explain what it feels like to go, round and round with death all around you. There is no other truth, war makes for unbelievable bonds between people. We tell lies to keep each other out of trouble. It is like a bunch of kids in summer camp together. At times we hold each other and cry about what we did not know. Some guys crack up a little and are held and rocked by their close friends. God we are so young. One guy from a little town in New York has never kissed a woman. How can we die and be so young?

Back at Subic Bay we find a cracked main beam, three compressors are out and a main turbine. The compressors operate the gun mounts. One rudder motor is out also and here we are fighting a war with all this stuff busted. We will have to spend some time in Subic for repairs, where the *Yardbirds* (shipyard workers) do all the work instead of our engineering people. I ask a couple of Bosun's Mates about the equipment and they know nothing. I keep quiet, but the *scuttlebutt* flies anyway and everyone thinks we might go home. The action has been so heavy we even go to General Quarters several times during our gunfire support stint. When the gyro compass fails, we stand a chance of going aground and will be a real easy target for the enemy. We have to get tugboats to pull us out of harm's way and wait until the gyro compass is repaired, which was not easy.

We start an anchor pool selling tickets for the exact time we will officially log into port, and the ante gets big, about one hundred and eighty dollars. We have three different hours and all the minutes. We are always trying to have some entertainment. The winner of the pool buys drinks for everybody at the Enlisted Men's Club. I often wonder what it is like at the Officer's Club and what they are up to over there. When we get back to Subic all the same girls are trying to get escorts on and off base and the same beer bottle-throwing bitch tries to coerce me to be her escort and I want nothing to do with it.

She keeps begging me to escort her and finally I have to yell at her and another beer bottle comes my way. Sanchez breaks the two of us up as I try to protect myself from her swinging arms and screams. I think she has experience with rejection. I did not even know her name.

Subic Bay has a nickname or two including, Shit City, Sin City, and the Asshole of the Earth. There is no recreation here except sex, drugs and, rock and roll. The bands are all fantastic and some guys want to bring them to the U.S. for tours. I bet they could make some money, but getting a visa was like pulling teeth. The place is a pervert's paradise. You can have anything you want and there is talk of pedophiles getting kids given to them.

In a couple of the clubs you can pay the hookers to pick up a quarter off the top of a beer bottle with their pussy. Right in the middle of the table with everyone watching. We are all in stress city, but looking back on it now, none of it was any good, including having such terrible hangovers we could hardly function.

After about one week in Subic, the repair schedule is extended and we are receiving more news about the peace treaty. We spend the time relaxing and playing cards at a bar called "Pee Wee's", a nice quiet place without live music.

On the tenth of December, I decide to bar-hop and travel to as many different places as I can. Leroy warns me to pair up with someone and watch for danger everywhere. I tell him I can take care of myself, but listen to him. Life is like cowboys and Indians for the Filipino's. My bar-hopping travels turn into a nightmare.

One of the bars I stop at, a bunch of drunken Sailors are paying for the quarter beer bottle game. I am watching from a few tables away. I see one of the drunken Sailors heat up the quarter with a lighter under the table, just hot enough for him to still be able to handle it. He puts it on the bottle and there is an excruciating scream as the woman picks it up with her pussy. In an instant, she takes out a knife, slices up his face, kicks him in the head, and tumbles him like a sack of shit. Not a moment of hesitation on her part. It only takes a few minutes for the MP's to arrive and the commotion starts. The MP's speak Tagalo and it is fast and furious. They call an ambulance for the guy with the slashed-up face. The hooker tries to make some sense of it all and none of us know what she is saying because of the language.

I am welded to my chair and afraid the MP's will just shoot every Sailor in the place. The girl is rolling around on the floor and screaming. The MP's have their guns drawn and the barkeep is obviously trying to explain the incident. I wish I had stayed at Pee Wee's where things were quiet. The ambulance arrives. The MP's decide not to do anything to anybody and let the girl go. It is all over in a flash. The military police here will just as soon shoot you, as take you in, it being easier to shoot and kill you.

"Dead men tell no tales!" Sure, is an appropriate saying. This is only the start of my adventure. I check into a hotel which has no windows, but does have a lock on the door. After midnight there is a big commotion, some guy has a hooker by the arm and will not let her go. I am shacked up and watching out of a second story window. The Sailor starts to beat on her, and the hooker kicks him. He is obviously fucked up on booze or drugs or both. He then starts to drag her and kick her, as the MP's arrive in a jeep. The MP's yell out something in Tagalo, and he kicks her again, paying no attention to the MP's.

Then it happens, the first death I have ever seen. An MP with a fifty-caliber mounted machine gun just opens up from about fifty feet away and blows the Sailor away. He crumbles to the ground like a piece of meat in a slaughterhouse. I could not watch anymore and I think of the words from the chief at Quarters, *"this is one of the most dangerous ports in the world"*. I stay up all night, because of the incident. I try to communicate with the broad, the desk had sent to my room, for no good reason. I mean, I did not ask for her or anything. She must have come with the price of the room or something. Sometimes, I still see the guy being gunned down in my dreams.

The next day there is a fire on the ship and it turns out to be arson, at least as far as the NIS is concerned. More sabotage from someone who thinks this will keep us out of the war zone.

On December thirteenth, we have a GQ early in the morning due to a bomb threat. Dogs are brought aboard along with the bomb squad and we are tied up most of the day. The search finds nothing, obviously some of the Filipinos do not like Americans and are sympathetic to the communist cause. We do not need to be in Vietnamese waters to have a lot of action going on.

The Doc has a talk about VD and much of the crew have sad faces. Nobody thought they could or would catch it for some reason. Some strains cannot be cured, and the men were taking chances with their life.

About twenty percent of the men get it and pay the price with a penicillin needle the size of Texas. Bend over and drop your pants as the Doc would say. He obviously is pissed off over so many men having VD.

The hooker I was with gave me my infection. I did not even want to have sex with her, but she just did a number on me, more or less raping me. I think she wanted to give me a case of whatever she had.

Neuman and I are on the road, when we meet of all things a couple of girls and one of them speaks perfect English. We are amazed. What amazes us even more is the fact they are runaways from another part of the islands and came to Subic as a last resort to escape the rigid Filipino lifestyle. Bob and I decide their real goal in escaping was to find a Sailor to marry, so they can get to the United States. The girls are very terrified of the MP'S, but we all have a lot of fun together.

The girls did not have hooker ID cards, which are issued by the government. Cora tell us about their friends who also ran away from home, and are picked up by the MP's, they are raped and beaten and forced into prostitution.

The girls are staying with a sister-in-law, who lives far from the Olongapo City limits in her own house, and she has a government job. There are no jobs anywhere and we wonder why they would want to leave home. Cora explains the lifestyle at home is no day at the beach, especially for girls.

Cora pulls up her blouse and shows us the marks on her back where her father had beat her with a strap just for suspecting she had been smoking pot. Not knowing which is worse, home or being in Olongapo, they are afraid to return home and afraid of the streets, being unsure where they should go.

Everyone speaks English at her sister-in-law's house and we have a fabulous time just getting along, drinking beer and talking about many things. We help them to speak better English and they seem grateful. We listen to Cora's brother playing guitar as we dine on native foods. I still think they thought one of us would marry them. I mean you could always get a divorce later after you got back to the states, but it would never happen, especially with me.

Monkeys chatter in the jungle from outside of the house and everybody feeds them, they are just like pets. After what happened with the hookers and the Sailor getting blown away by the MP's, being here is like paradise. The repairs to the ship are finished and we will be leaving for the war zone in the next day or so, just in time for Christmas.

Dolly, who is Cora's friend, takes a liking to me and wants to go to Manila. We take the trip on a rickety old bus overflowing with people and carrying live animals in the back. We spend most of the night traveling. The MP's stop the bus a few times and Dolly warns me to pretend I do not know her or the MP's might get suspicious. Manila is clean with beautiful scenery of mostly jungle.

The time to leave nears and I feel the fear overwhelm me again. I do not want to go back to Vietnam. Dolly is crying every now and then for seemingly no reason. When I ask her what is wrong, she tells me she is sad about being in a bad situation and fears the MP's. I am in love again and do not know what to do. I feel like going AWOL and seeking a job in Manila and never going home again. The thoughts hit me and I wake up to reality.

Leroy and I go over to the EM Club the day before departure. He tells me sea stories about how many loves he has left behind in how many ports. Nothing a few bottles of beer with friends will not cure. Leroy drinks me under the table and I pass out somewhere on the ship. Leroy is like a father figure to all of us in the HT shop even to the older guys. Leroy is black and no one seems to care as prejudice is only a word. Anytime something is bothering you, he will listen and seems to take it in stride. He is cool as a cucumber.

The entire crew goes bananas as an announcement is made at Quarters for Muster and Inspection on about the tenth of November. The Chief seems in disbelief as he reads it, but did his best.

"Men there has been an executive order issued from Admiral Elmo Zumwalt, the Commander in Chief of the Navy."

"There have been concerns over racial issues and he has issued an executive order to be followed by all the ships in the entire Navy. All ships shall elect a Race Relations Coordinator and this coordinator shall be in charge of any issues that are deemed to be of a racial nature. The Race Relations Coordinator, shall have the power to supersede the Captain in these issues and shall have the authority to have his commands be of a higher authority than the Commander of the vessel. Firstly, it must be determined to be of a racial nature for the coordinator to intercede. Secondly this shall be an elected position and the entire crew shall vote upon the matter. Whomever is elected is expected to do the job as a mediator and work things out."

Leroy shouts out.

"I want to nominate Nardone and I want to do it now."

There is grumbling and chatter among the men.

The Chief responds.

"It is possible for Nardone to be nominated. We can take the vote now and make it a matter of official record."

I shout.

"What the hell are you doing, Leroy! I don't know anything about doing this kind of stuff and you want to nominate me to have more power than the Captain."

Leroy feels I am best suited for the job and he stands by his desire to nominate me and there is nothing I can do about it.

"All right everybody is there any objections to the nomination of Petty Officer Nardone for the position of Race Relations Coordinator?"

No one objects and the chief asks for a show of hands from the men as to the yeas and everybody raises their hands, then a messenger is sent to the fo'c'sle to inform them and ask for their vote. They all agree. There is not one objection and I become the Race Relations Coordinator.

I ask the Chief if there are any guidelines for the position, because I have absolutely no idea as to what I will do and he tells me there aren't any.

Our departure is delayed another two days due to engine problems and I wonder what else can go wrong. The entire crew is nervous and edgy. We still have cold iron watches in all compartments and there will be no last night liberty. Well at least there will be no hangovers. *Scuttlebutt* is flying around about someone sabotaging the engines. The Captain is furious and wants to give extra duty to everyone aboard.

Bobo and Kelly are playing practical jokes on everybody, like kids at a summer camp. The entire crew knows deep down inside this ship is not fit for action and it just makes the fear worse. I miss Dolly and realize many men left women behind in Charleston and how they must feel. We are all patched up and ready to go. We are scheduled to spend thirty days on the gun line. We may be on the gun line for Christmas or maybe we will get some "R and R", in a Vietnamese port somewhere.

I receive a letter from home with rumors of the war ending soon. I receive some newspaper clippings about Vietnam. Nixon will announce a treaty soon, something I really did not want to read about, all the heavy fighting by Marines, the deaths and the body counts. What was my mother thinking anyway?

We are back on the gun line with the same old routine of Beep! Beep! Boom! Standing watch six on and six off. The word continues to be passed.

"All hands stand clear of the main decks while taking hostile fire."

You know like we are just going to run out there and try to get a look at the war zone.

On the mess decks a radioman I am eating with tells all at the tables, heavy armament is coming into the VC and NVA and a destroyer has been sunk, along with two more tin cans taking extensive damage on the gun line. We all hope that it is only *scuttlebutt*. Hoping it is just a story, not wanting to think about it, but why would he make it up? There are never any answers from the Engineering Officer for our questions.

Bobo shows me a place, during a nighttime illumination run. We bribe the supply clerk to look out of a hole in the bulkhead in the supply office. Staring through the hole we can see the action, the one and only time I did. I watch as the Willie Peter rounds fired from the ship light up the night sky like crazy. I cannot believe how bright they are. I hear the shells whistle through the air and explode above the ground, knowing how many seconds the rounds are set for from standing the gun mount watches. Bobo and I are like little children exposing something forbidden. My only glimpse of the war and I could have done without it. I imagine guys running around and trying to fight with the illumination being their only light. My imagination made it real.

The next day is quiet and just before the truce for Christmas. We all know what is going on around us, and yet we seem to deny it. All of us are locked up tight, except the personnel on the bridge and George in the directional control bubble outside and we play cards as the guns go off. We are all tired and drinking loads of coffee. The Doc tells the crew at quarters, not to drink too much coffee as it can actually cause a psychosis. Walking by each other in the passageway we all look like zombies with wide-open and bloodshot eyes, kind of shuffling our feet, unable to pick them up. Then the fear sets in and we are ready for action as all hell and will run when the word is passed at General Quarters, this is not a DRILL!

I go down into main control every day to visit Neuman while he is on watch. He does not like what we are doing and tells me he is sick just thinking about me setting the fuses and working the death squad. I tell him his attitude sucks and he should look at it like a group effort. I tell him I have to go stand my 1800-2400 watch. He is not off-duty until 2000.

On the aft gun mount watch I have the headphones on, setting the fuses for point detonation, all of a sudden, a screaming voice comes over the headphones. "Cease fire! Cease fire! Assholes, you have just killed about eighteen Marines!" Your coordinates screwed up or what. I could only think of George up in fire control and what he must be going through.

How could I set another fuse? How could I continue? We have just committed an act of "Friendly Fire", as they call it and it haunts me to this day? I remember it as if it happened a week ago. What if I had set the fuses wrong and that was the problem. I could not remember what the fuse setting was supposed to be. I could not sleep for days between the guns going off and thinking of this incident. I just walk around like a zombie and chain-smoke my brains out. George told me that it is all in the coordinates and had nothing to do with the setting of the fuses and that I should not worry about it anymore.

We are still on Naval Gunfire Support and one day word comes over the IC (Interior Communication System) from the forward gun mount, a shell has gotten stuck in the barrel of the gun mount. What the hell if it was set for a timing it would have blown up in the barrel. They cool down the barrel and somehow get the shell out, I do not know how.

Our mission shifts to rescue and assistance, which involves our ship shadowing a carrier in the event a plane has to ditch then search for the pilot and rescue him. We are also allowed outside at this point, since we are beyond the nine-mile limit, which is the range of the guns from shore, so I take a few pictures. I wonder if they actually have guns with more than a range of nine miles. We are set to anchor in Danang for three days of rest from the NGFS.

The Captain informs us we are not allowed to leave the ship and does not give us a reason for it. Here we all are, aboard ship with holiday routine for the next three days. The Marine Commander at Danang outranks the Captain, although even he cannot get us off the ship, but he does pull a fast one and gets permission for the Marines to come aboard and chat. The crew makes arrangements for the Marines to use the showers and take Hollywood's (A nickname for a shower that lasts as long as you want it to).

The Marines bring a wheelbarrow full of dirt and dump it on the fantail. They spread the word over the 1MC, "Anyone who wants to step foot in Vietnam can come to the fantail and visit with the Marines." The Marines set-up their own watch rotation and have the Sailors step on the dirt in a ritualistic fashion, like kids playing a game. They all take their Hollywood's and thank us a lot.

We are given time off, due to the weather being rough as hell. We are bouncing all over the place with a starboard list of fifteen degrees and a port side list of twenty-five degrees. The end of the year is near and a few men joke about having spent two years in Nam.

I remember something that happened during Christmas mail detail. I wrote about it in my diary and something happened years later that was so ironic, even I could not believe it happened. In an Elks club in the late 1970's after being discharged. I am drinking with some older man who is about the age of my father. We are telling stories of being in the military and life in general. I talk about the Navy and my tour of Vietnam. A friend of my father tells us his son was aboard USS Higbee which took a hit in Danang Harbor on Christmas day in 1972. I explain to him how I had begged to go over to the Higbee on Christmas day to see a friend and remember the whole thing. We are unloading Christmas mail on the fantail and sorting it for distribution to other ships who would then send over motor whaleboats to pick-up the cherished mail. I was being all pissy, because I am denied permission to go over to the Higbee and since it is Christmas maybe they could show some compassion. We are supposed to be under a cease-fire for the holiday. There are Sampans all over Danang harbor and the Higbee was only about one hundred yards away from our ship. They start hoisting up the motor whaleboat as guys are waiting and watching the mail detail.

Then it happened, *Blam! Blam!* The whole thing blows apart with bodies flying all over the place. The whole boat just disintegrates into a million pieces. We are ordered to stand by in case they need Damage Control help. On the Higbee, men are running all over the place, their mail is gone and all their friends too. No one on our ship can tell where the RPG had come from and the guys just start using the fifty calibers on any sampan in sight without asking permission. They are stopped quickly by Petty Officer First Class Leroy, as he yells, we do not want any innocent people killed. In my opinion the rocket must have come from one of those Sampans.

Memories of the killing of my Marine comrades by friendly fire or the Higbee incident, I do not know which one was worse or more intense. I groaned and grumbled about being denied permission to go over to the Higbee by the Captain, which kept me alive and it was the first time that I actually liked him.

Those rotten commies had planned it all so it would have psychological impact during what was supposed to be a cease-fire. We were all just standing on the side of the ship watching. We sent our whaleboat over to assist in recovery of the bodies, of course the Higbee no longer had one to search with.

After the Higbee incident, an anchor watch is instituted to make sure the Sampans do not get too close to the ship, along with special security watches staffed by gunner's mates armed with forty-five caliber pistols, who will stand watch with the sounding and security men. One of the guys in "R" Division receives some screwed-up Christmas mail, a letter with no return address and he wonders where it comes from. He opens it and there are photographs of dead Marines with their dicks cut off and stuck into their mouths. He just stares at the photos.

I stare at the photographs blankly and tell him.

"Don't you know how much the enemy knows about us? You are receiving mail and they know who you are. Now give me those pictures and stop showing them around."

"Don't you realize this is psychological warfare? These commie bastards are sharp to every facet of war and these pictures are just another example of what they will do to make it worse."

I took the pictures to the Engineering Officer and he did something with them. I would have burned them.

There is another incident where a Sampan threw a satchel bag onto the deck of the ship and not knowing if it contained explosives or not, we are told to get out the fire hoses and wash the satchel over the side and then push it away from the ship. No one knew if the satchel bag

72

contained a bomb or not, luckily it did not explode.

We leave out of Danang and back to the big war for more NGFS. The guns on the ship fire so much that we have to cool down the barrels again.

There is a special announcement at Quarters for muster and Inspection by the chief.

"Men we are going up to Haiphong Harbor and participating in Operation Linebacker. We have to load up on ammo and be ready. This is supposed to be the big push to end the war and we will see some heavy action. Haiphong is the most heavily fortified port in all of warfare's history and we need to be ready."

He stops and clears his throat.

"I know that some of you have not been wearing your dog tags and this is mandatory, there will be an inspection tomorrow at Quarters. We could be taken, as POW's and you definitely want to have your dog tags on your ass. We will be spending some more time on NGFS and then we should leave for North Vietnam about the third of January. There will be holiday routine for New Year's Day. That is all and there are no questions to answer. We will really be in the midst of combat."

We are still on NGFS, but now there is a new pattern. The ship steams in close to provoke attack by shore batteries, then we call in the coordinates to the Navy pilots, who attempt counter attack and we just steam away while the aircraft do the bombing. We do not return fire. We go out to refuel and then go right back into the zone again. The holiday routine approaches and we all cannot wait.

I am called upon for my first duty as the Race Relations Coordinator. There is a dispute between some of the officers and I am asked to talk over the problem with all the First Class Petty Officers and the Chiefs. There is a problem between a redneck Chief from Georgia and a black Chief from a northern state.

The redneck, a Gunner's Mate, who is a pain in the ass, seems to think the black Chief, an Engineer takes advantage of his stature, does not clean up after himself or shower enough. He even complains that the black Chief leaves beard clippings in the sink. The Chief, from the state of Georgia, does not have the respect of his men and he is a slob. Believing it is a case of jealousy, I speak my mind and tell both of them it is in their upbringing to hate each other and they will have to get along. I decide they both must meet with me for half an hour every day to work out their differences.

These two men are ready to get into a fight and that would have been disastrous for both of their careers. I think I did a hell of a job working with them.

I went to the XO and resigned my Race Relations Position. I tell them I can't do it anymore, because there are no guidelines for the position and it is difficult dealing with the men.

The XO makes the announcement at Quarters for Muster and Inspection.

"Men, Petty Officer Third Class Nardone has resigned as the elected Race Relations Coordinator – what should we do?

Leroy Sass steps out of line and confronts me.

"What the hell are you doing Nardone?"

"I am quitting the job!"

Leroy points a finger at me and says.

"I will not let you quit."

He meanders around and around, speaking loudly.

"What should we do guys, what can we do?"

One of the men breaks ranks and steps in front of Leroy, and he starts to chant loudly.

"We want Nardone! We want Nardone!"

He throws his clenched fists in the air and continues to chant, then all the Sailors suddenly join in the the chant with their fists in the air.

"We Want Nardone!"

I do not know how or why, but a Sailor comes running down the side of the ship and approaches the Chiefs and the Officers.

"We have been informed by the Bosun's Mate that all the men on the fo'c'sle section for Quarters are chanting for Nardone."

A Sailor from the forward post also comes to join the chant.

The Chiefs and the Officers point at me with a stern looking repetitive cocking of their pointed fingers.

I start to shout and raise my hands as high as I can, while I scream,

"I Will do it! I will do it!"

There are many handshakes and back-slapping as the Chief yells loudly.

"Okay! Okay! Let's get back to order and discipline. Tell the men on the fo'c'sle and the forward post what has happened."

When Quarters is over, I talk with Mike.

It is a bitch after all those escapist days on leave in Olongapo City, outside of Subic Bay to be in the war zone. Sanchez talks to me and is concerned about my excessive drinking and smoking pot. He tells me I am not nice when I am drunk and should think about quitting both the dope and the beer.

"Mike you know it is the tension and the war that makes me drink. I can tell you that I almost never came back from Manila. I would have stayed there except for what EJ told me about what happens if you go AWOL. He had been to the brig and I sure as hell did not want to go. I'm scared like all of us and I cannot cope so I use the booze and the drugs as a crutch."

"Oh, my poor friend, Nardone. Can't you see that it just makes matters worse? You cannot escape where you are. We are all afraid, the men like us who read all the work requests and damage control reports are like everybody else. Then you, Bobo, and a couple of the guys wander around griping and bitching, telling everybody how bad it is and acting like nobody else knows how much we are all going through, after a while nobody can stand listening to you and Bobo. I've got to tell you it is time for you to stop bitching, and get on with life. I left a wife behind, which isn't a day at the beach."

"Hey Mike what can I do? I am not the same happy-go-lucky kid who enlisted over a year ago. We killed those Marines and I am still haunted by it. I probably will be haunted the rest of my life. Every time I set the fuses, I can hear the screams of the men and see the bodies being blown apart."

"Nardone everybody has to deal with it."

Mike sighed.

"Nardone, people would not have asked me to talk to you if they did not like you. You do know some of the Puerto Ricans respect you, because you bothered to learn to speak Spanish? But you blow hot and cold, one minute you are calm and then at the drop of a hat you pounce on people and get crazy. I am telling you this for your own good."

I did not know what to say.

"Mike, I have been keeping a diary, writing in it every day and would like to read something to you. Let's go to the rear penthouse and chat for a while."

"Sounds good, Nardone, you go get some coffee and I will get some blankets to sit on."

It was a hot balmy night and the seas were extremely calm. Mike, me and other guys would treat it as a ritual, having those one on one rap sessions and letting it all hang out. Other men would come by and ask what we were doing. Mike would tell them that we wanted to be alone. The visitors would crack a joke about our sexual preferences and we would tell them to fuck off and leave us alone.

Another guy stops by and asks us if he can stay and rap awhile. We said why the hell not! Sometime later there were seven of us on the rear gun mount just telling stories and getting down with it, by the sea and all the tranquility. I must have read from my diary twenty times and Mike knew who to ask to stay and who to ask to leave. He was like a coach of a team or something. A few days later, I realize these are the guys who had talked to Sanchez with their concerns about my behavior. The men's caring and concern led them to support me, letting me blow off steam and biting the bullet about their own fears. Mike had actually asked them to come by while he was getting the blankets. I am being a bastard and these guys are showing up to tell me about it in their own ways. I read the ode from my diary over and over to each person who stopped by.

The flash of fire outside, you know it glows. Even though in this gray hulk it can only be heard. Just like our brotherhood it is an unseen reality. All the Sailors out at sea they must all feel like me. We are all here not there and our feelings we must share. There is no escape not to use booze or drugs. Only in our minds eye can we see home and mom's apple pie. Our hands they shake, and it ain't, like John Wayne in the, 'Red Witches Wake.' We try to be bold but some of us hold onto reality by a thin thread. We must admit that the roads of war we fear to tread. Our lives are lost if we cannot complain, someone will go insane. Give me a gun and the jungle. The right to see my enemy. Anything but locked up tight my fists clenched white with fright. Waiting for the rockets to hit. All we can do is sit and sit and sit. Sometimes I cannot take a shit waiting for that rocket to hit. We are at the fringes of the war zone floating in and out. What is it all about? We steam here and we steam there, all of us lost without our deepest thoughts to share. We dream of this gray beast sinking in the sea. Who will be lost me or him? You cannot escape the reality. Give me the gun and the jungle to fend for myself. I'd rather die there than sitting out at sea. Sometimes I want to crack, have them take me away, but always thoughts of my brothers make me stay. The peace talk news brings the adrenaline through, but when it does not happen, I know I will die before those political assassins sign it. How can I write what I feel, there is nothing but the men and the sea. You cannot escape the reality. All of us together can help us deal with our worst enemy, OURSELVES.

The guys liked my prose or so they said.

Are we men or boys?

We head back to Subic Bay before leaving for Operation Linebacker.

There I meet a man at the Base Exchange, who graduated from boot camp with me. Albert Thomas, a religious man from a small town down South and he was dirt poor. The military was his only escape. He takes me on a tour of the United States ultimate fighting ship the USS America (CV-66) an eighty thousand tons, Kitty Hawk-class supercarrier. There are five times as many men on the carrier as lived in his hometown. I ask him how he is adapting. He took me from the highest to the lowest decks, telling me how many stories it was. There is even a movie theater. The top of our mast did not even reach the flight deck of that monster. Thomas told me all about the missions they had gone on and how they all watch the nightly news via satellite. There are five thousand men aboard, some he will never meet. They are tight with each other within their own divisions.

We talk about how different it is on a Destroyer, a smaller ship with a smaller crew, who all knew each other.

The crew on the carrier uses coffee at the rate of about two hundred and fifty pounds per day, a main priority for the men, just like on my ship. We laugh and want to switch places with each other for a few days.

He tells me about a woman he had met at church in Olongapo and how he wants to marry her. We both had our lovers, mine was Dolly and I really liked her a lot.

"Albert, what will you do when you take her home to the hellhole you come from? Maybe you should make the Navy your career."

"I just might Nardone, there is no better place for me. My wife would be more comfortable with the other Filipinos that are in the Navy, than being in my hometown."

"She is still from another world and that is all I know, Albert."

We both felt we could overcome all odds by taking the chance of getting married to a woman that we had found in the city of Olongapo. The hookers fell to their knees sometimes begging you to marry them and take them away from the life they were leading. They would do anything to please you and be a good wife. Then I realize, how could somebody marry a hooker from this shit-hole?

We are our own worst enemies and hated the thought of not getting an easy woman. Sanchez would be yelling and screaming, telling me to get it together and not to do anything rash. Dolly had said she was a college student and all, but was that really true? What difference does it make? She is still a Filipino. My true love, Dolly, lived on the edge of Olongapo. I would stay overnight with the roaches and rats all over the place and let's not forget the lizards. After all the incidents with the animals and the insects, I swore I would never go back again. I told Dolly that I would be staying on the ship from now on.

We are on another visit to Subic Bay for more repairs. It seems as if all we do is get repairs to the ship. A Marine mentions Olongapo is as close to Saigon as you can get and knows because he has been there. I feel the souls of the men who are in-country and talk with many who are coming to Olongapo via ships used for transporting the troops. Even though we are leaving for Operation Linebacker, we still have one more run of Naval Gunfire Support and it is a *doozy*. We take damage to the aft of the ship, and I find out any shell that does damage is considered to be a direct hit as far as official records go.

I receive letters from home with, *We Pray for Peace!* emblazoned on the outside. Hell, I pray to live, and peace must come soon.

On our last NGFS I go a little nutty and start beating on the shell saying there is a nub on it and it will never fly right and we have to get this nub off. Yacus (Butch) grabs my hand and asks what the hell is wrong with me.

I answer.

"I still cannot get those Marines out of my mind, Butch and it bothers me every day."

"This shell is good enough to kill whoever we are trying to kill Nardone and that is that. Take it easy and just do your job and set the fuses!"

"You know Butch we only have one more day and then we are going up north to Haiphong. I cannot wait to see what it is like."

Right in the middle of a bombing run, the Main malfunctions, and we are unable to fire a round. I hope the ship does not get hit with shells while we are on NGFS, wondering if the ship is in good enough shape to stand up to the war. The waves are going over the second deck and it is rough. I go to the bridge and am told something I do not want to hear. What is could be worse the weather or the war?

We are on the way to Haiphong and Arroyo passes me a note to speak with him after his watch is over. I am on sounding and security watch and will get off at the same time he does. We meet as arranged and he tells me about a big storm right in our path and that we do not have enough fuel to make any changes in course, he also finds out the fuel numbers do not match. The logbook shows the fuel we took on in Subic does not match the amount of fuel that we have aboard and we will have to take the storm head on. Why the hell don't the numbers match? I ask. Arroyo believes there is something illegal going on and does not know what it is. I make note of this in my diary and remember to tell the Engineering Officer about it.

Leroy tells me not to tell the Engineering Officer about the discrepancy. I believe it has something to do with a welding job where I was standing fire watch for Leroy. We kept burning holes in the side of the ship as we tried to weld a metal patch to the bulkhead. I keep making bigger pieces and they do not work. Leroy keeps burning holes in the side of the ship. Later in the day he tells me, with nobody else around, that the records show this section of the hull was one inch thick and the hull should not be burning through at this spot. He suspects foul play and tells me to keep my mouth shut and not tell anyone about it. Leroy believes the ships records might be falsified.

We will be in North Vietnamese waters in around two days if we can take the storm. We receive mail from a helicopter and my father writes something in a letter, which I copy in my diary.

"No one would be foolish enough to choose war over peace - in peace sons bury their fathers, but in war fathers bury their sons." - Croesus of Lydia.

*Illustration 5: Petty Officer Third Class
Pedro Arroyo - Electronic Counter
Measures*

This piece of prose has an effect on me. Just like on the envelopes - *We Pray for Peace!* I feel as if the war has been on the news so long that nobody seems to think it is real, or do they believe the fighting is as bad as other wars. Letters from home showed how much everyone really cared, but I never told them how scared and scarred by the war I was. I did not want to expose them to our torment. I did not want to bury anybody. I just want to live through it all. The poem just enhances my fears.

An announcement comes over the 1MC.

"Men we have been called to duty on a special mission and will have to make a full power run to Quang Tri. There is a report of a division of NVA (North Vietnamese Army) on the way there and we have been called to offer fire support for the South Vietnamese. This will require a lot from everybody and this ship has not seen a full power run in a long time and it will get hairy. We sure are glad we took on extra fuel from that tanker or we would not be able to go to our appointed place of duty."

We are at full power, full speed of about twenty-four knots, which is about thirty-five miles per hour and I think to myself is this even possible. The ship shudders and vibrates. We all wait for the ship to totally disintegrate as we receive notice that the North Vietnamese Army (NVA) has retreated and rumors are it was because we were on our way there to assist with Naval Gunfire Support. The news makes us bold and boisterous thinking of how the enemy had retreated because the NVA knew the "Bad Ass Navy" was on the way.

Then we get some unexpected news via the 1MC.

"Men the trip to Haiphong has been put on hold for now and we are going to take time to pull into Hong Kong for some "R and R". Everybody is guaranteed to get one overnight liberty."

With this news we are like children who have been denied candy for months.

Hong Kong is supposed to be one of the most heavily populated areas in the entire world. We have to anchor in the harbor and take junks to the pier. We are warned not to go alone on the junks, because you could get robbed and *fed to the fish*. We heed the warning and go over in groups. We stay at the Hotel Kennedy, because it is supposed to be Sailor friendly and has a military discount.

Six of us rent a three-bedroom suite with a Jacuzzi tub, two bathrooms and double beds in each room. The price is decent and we go everywhere together. The city is difficult to deal with, because it is so crowded. I call home from the base telephone exchange, which consists of a giant area with individual telephones in small open booths. The call is expensive and my father is happy to hear from me but wonders about the cost of the call, so we only talk for a short time.

I talk about cooling off the barrels and waiting to be fired upon before returning fire and this is about all I tell him about the war. All I want to do is take a hot bubble bath and have a hamburger. I could do with a woman, and in the hotel room they have a directory of females to call. It sure is a different type of world. I pray that we will never have to return to "Operation Linebacker".

Hong Kong is divided up into three sections including, a French section, a British section, and a Swedish section. We are told to avoid the Swedish section, so naturally we go there. The Swedes keep bothering us and tell us to leave their women alone. The women are supposedly more beautiful in the Swedish section and they sure were nice. We do not have any problems, which is good. We head for the British section and go to a good Seafarers bar which Mengel and Stearns had heard about from some *scuttlebutt* on the junk they took to the pier.

Englishmen will like us and treat us right. Twenty of us go there and take up a lot of space.

We listen to the jukebox and ponder our future. The English Merchant Marines are all dressed *seawise* with boots, pea coats, and watch caps. It was a real heave-ho! We order some pitchers of beer and some of us go to the bar to talk to the "Brits". The bar is full and the music is loud. After Stearns and Leroy talk at the bar for a while the jukebox volume lowers and a couple of the "Brits" raise their mugs and shout above the noise.

"Let's hear it fellows, a toast and a tune to our American friends."

In unison they bellow.

"Here's to the warriors of the high seas, keep on fighting and bring those commies to their knees!"

Then they begin singing some *sea ditty* about long lost love.

Then the "Brits" repeat the toast.

"Here's to the warriors of the high seas, keep on fighting and bring those commies to their knees!"

They buy all of us drinks and we mingle at the bar together. After word got back to the ship all the guys wanted to go to the "Yellow Submarine Bar".

The next night we party again and are walking back to the pier, when we see a friend "go down". There are some strange insurance laws in Hong Kong and they would rather kill you than step on the brakes. Roy wanted to leave us and go get a hooker. He was very drunk and wandered away. We wished him well and reminded him that we were told to stay in groups. We tried to get him to go back to the ship with us but he would have nothing to do with it. He wanted a hooker and a hotel room. He got belligerent and acted like a typical drunken Sailor. He walked away and we started our trip back to the pier. All of a sudden you could hear the sound of the brakes on the pavement and we turned to see him get hit by a cab. He flew a long distance in the air and we did not know if we should get involved or not.

Stearns tells us.

"If we get involved as witnesses, they will keep us and we cannot afford to as the ship is supposed to leave in the morning."

Stearns has been in the Navy for eighteen years and everyone trusts his opinion.

"He is just a drunken Sailor and died at the fringes of the war zone."

I ask, how do we know if he is dead? Stearns said, that if he wasn't dead, he would go to the hospital ship in the harbor. They made the announcement the next day at quarters. Roy had multiple contusions, broken bones and a fractured skull. He was aboard the hospital ship and his condition was poor. They did not expect him to make it through the next couple of days

"Well at least he isn't aboard this ship and going up to the North."

Bill Rudek mumbles.

"Well I would rather be here than where he is. At least we don't have any physical injuries only psychological ones so far. You are nuts, Rudek and always will be."

"Nardone, this is only a pit stop, I would not doubt it if he walked in front of the cab on purpose. I knew him really well and I think he did it purposefully to get out of this world. I mean like suicide you know. He has been talking about it to me lately in our personal conversations."

I pay fifty dollars to check out a woman from a club and we do not even have sex. Sanchez and I ask for someone who can speak English. We go to a club called "Maxim's", supposedly one of the best club's in the world and we are not disappointed. The woman tries to teach us to eat with chopsticks and it sure as hell is funny or at least she thinks so. We go over to her house and lounge around watching television with what else, but more war news.

One of my favorite television shows, "Combat" is on with Vic Morrow speaking Chinese with subtitles in English. I thought of the way the show had affected me as a kid growing up and watching it. They were all heroes killing the Germans, and winning the war. I watched every week and thought that I could be a hero just like the characters on the show. It was a farce and nowhere near the truth. They were blowing up Germans and speaking Chinese. It seemed like a comedy show. She changes the channel back to the news.

We watch and wonder where we will be in a few weeks. Then *Blam!* it hits, a report on the news in English about ships that have taken heavy damage at Quang Tri with pictures and all. They show the holes blown into the sides of the ships and the war is there for us to watch and see where we will be going. I am more afraid now than I have been, there it is on the news with a casualty list and all. I have been denying it all along thinking nothing could happen to us. Everything changes with us as we watch the news.

She speaks to us in English and we tell her we are going back to the war zone in a couple of days. We leave during the night and return to the ship. She asks for money and I give her some.

News came again as we prepare to leave Hong Kong. We would be steaming right up North into all the action. The Captain repeated his words of warning.

"Men - this is the Captain, speaking. We are going up north for bombing runs and the action will be heavy. The B-52's will be bombing Hanoi and we will be on the attack at Haiphong. The harbor is mined and not many ships make the trip because of this. We expect stiff resistance and believe that the North Vietnamese know we are coming. A lot of you have not been wearing your dog tags and there will be an inspection at quarters tomorrow. Everyone must have them on. There is a possibility that we may have to abandon ship and if that happens you definitely want your dog tags on. We will start steaming north tomorrow at 1100 hours and the rest will go down in the history books. Keep your wits about you and that is all for now."

All I want to do is smoke a big joint and forget everything going on, but instead Sanchez, me and a few guys go to the rear penthouse and rap. Some guys read their poetry and some share their "Dear John" letters from home. One guy wrote about how we were just as brave as any Marine. He told us a story about being beaten up by a bunch of Marines in Subic Bay and he was too embarrassed to go to sickbay, so he just lived with the pain both emotional and physical. He had lived with it and just now dumped it out on the group. He was only seventeen years old and I felt very sorry for him. Why did Marines do things like that?

We talk about ourselves and the deep feelings we have for others in the group and aboard in general. We are really a tight crew thus the expression, "Tin Can Tight". It is like saying prayers only without the Amen.

We have already been through a lot and have seen all kinds of things happen in just a short time. We have been in the War Zone since before Thanksgiving and now we are in the heaviest action of the war.

I am still standing sounding and security watches and it is relatively easy. I have the added duty of being the Race Relations Coordinator and ask many questions as I stand my watch and recon the entire ship. One night as I am standing watch, it hits the fan and scares the shit out of me. A black Sailor that I hardly knew jumps me and puts a nine-inch knife to my throat.

He tells me.

"Keep your cool and do not do anything dumb or I will slit your throat for sure. I want to lead a mutiny and I have a lot of Sailors that want to come with me. They will stay in the Philippines forever and never want to go home. I am taking you to the bridge, so let's go."

He leads me to the bridge and tries to take command of the ship with the loaded forty-five caliber pistol he has taken away from me and threatens to shoot the entire bridge staff if they do not immediately change course and go to Subic Bay.

One of the officers talks him out of it. There is so much tension, it scares me more than the war. What can a Sailor be thinking when he believes he can start a mutiny and everybody will come with him. He encounters one big problem, when he forces them to pass the word over the 1MC that he is taking command of the ship and nobody shows up. He is there all alone.

The officer who talks him out of his dilemma, confiscates the gun and calls for the Master at Arms to come to the bridge. The Master at Arms takes him away in handcuffs, but we have no place to secure him. They handcuff him to a pipe and have him sit in a chair until we get to Subic, where the Navy MP'S take him away. I was relieved of my watch and Sanchez has to stand the rest of it, while I give a statement to the Master at Arms. I explain the incident to him just as it went down and he acts like it was all my fault. I am mad and say.

"What did you expect me to do? Give him a kick and karate my way out of it. He had a nine-inch knife at my throat and I was not in the mood to argue. He was stressed out like crazy and he was not thinking right. I could have been killed and he could have killed somebody else. The officer on the bridge deserves a lot of credit, if not a commendation for his actions."

I ask to be excused, saying there was no more for me to say and I have given you a statement to the best of my abilities. I am released and left for the rear penthouse, hoping that someone would be there to talk to. A radioman stops up at the top of the gun mount and tells us the port of Haiphong is heavily fortified and filled with mines and we may have a mine watch. We steam at a slow speed to avoid a mine collision. On a few occasions the watch has to push off the mines with long poles. The Damage Control teams stand by and the crew is informed to be ready for General Quarters at a moment's notice

Then it finally comes. The word is passed.

General Quarters! General Quarters! This is not a drill! This is not a drill!

The faces of the men and the smells of the gear locker will always be with me. Leroy is our team leader and Grandpa leads a team too, the old drunk that he is. Smells waft of ropes, kerosene lamps and old stuff. OBA'S are worn by a few, short for Oxygen Breathing Apparatus and you must use them to fight fires. I wear mine all the time.

I have to take it off though when word comes over the 1MC that we have lost power in Bravo 3 and believe it is a steam leak of the 600-PSI steam which drives the shafts. They already have evacuated the hole, when I find out that nobody knows what to do except me due to my training in Class "A" School. The 600-PSI can cut through most anything and there is no protective clothing or anything like that. You have to take a broom and move it around you in a motion that will let you know where the steam leak is. The broom has to be moved exactly right and it is the most fear I have ever felt. We are under a heavy bombing attack and it is necessary to get the steam pressure back again. I grab the broom and start my descent down the ladder moving it around in a circle.

You must remember where you place the broom and be super careful. I find the leak about halfway down the ladder by hearing the hissing noise hitting the broom. I am overjoyed that the leak may be so close and I will not have to do the entire hole with the broom. I have hopefully found the one and only leak. I ask for assistance and Grandpa an EM2 comes down and I tell him to go stand on the side of the ladder on a gangway and bring the tools with him. I call up to Leroy, that I have found the broken valve and it is only a 600-PSI metal gasket between two parts. I can fix it if the machinists can make another gasket of steel or maybe I am hoping, there is a spare part or something. I ask Grandpa to move and hand me certain tools and he does not move.

"What the hell is wrong with you?" I ask him.

Grandpa responds.

"I am too scared to move and I am frozen in one spot."

"Set the tool bag down on the gangway, and if you cannot move, you will have to stay there."

The leak is on the left side of the ladder and I move cautiously knowing that one wrong move and I will be sliced up by the steam. I go down the gangway and step over the spot using the broom to let me know again where the leak is. I will have to turn off the steam from both sides of the leak and remove the whole damn valve.

I take a wrench, after shutting down the steam and remove the valve. After what seems like an eternity, I receive word from the Machine Shop that they will be able to manufacture the part needed. While this is happening, you can hear the ... Ping! Ping! Noise of the close hits nearby to the ship and we can only make about eight knots speed with the steam pressure down in Bravo 3.

Finally, the part arrives and I do my best to remain calm and replace it. I turn the valves on both sides and check with the broom to see if there is still a leak. Word comes from Main Control that the pressure is back up again, so the repair must have worked. I tell Grandpa he can move now and I use the broom on the way out of the hole, just in case.

The men return to duty in Bravo 3 to assume their watches. I go back to the gear locker and let out a scream of relief.

The men sit and talk about this being the real thing. We just know it is hot and we are going in on runs and firing the cannons. You can still hear the constant ... Ping! Ping! Due to the continuing close hits nearby the ship and it is enough to frighten anyone to death. The bulkheads rock and vibrate as the lights flicker. The load suddenly drops and everything goes black. I Sure as hell hope we can fix it fast, with the dropping of the main power we are dead in the water and cannot move.

As I reflect on how amazing it is that there has not been a direct hit to the bridge or anywhere else, word comes over the 1MC, we have taken a hit in the amidships region and it needs repair. The repair party members and I use a mattress and two by fours to brace a piece of plywood against the hull where the water is coming in. The mattress acts like a sponge and covers the holes better than anything else will.

The bulkheads shake as the shelling increases. There is a small peephole in the bulkhead and I can see fires glowing on the sea, planes in the sky and ships everywhere. We are definitely putting on a big push to force the North Vietnamese to sign the Peace Treaty and end the war. A guy named Randy starts to hum. Eventually it leads to all of us holding hands and singing, *'Onward Christian Soldiers'* and a few other songs which we all knew. Shouting comes from down in Main Control that a boiler has come loose from its foundation. There is nothing we can do, except try to brace it up with wood as water is coming in everywhere.

It is hotter than hell, we are all sweating and wonder if we will make it through all of this. There is more yelling and we have split some seams in the supply hold and we have to shore them up with plywood and mattresses also. The seams are cracking and the bombs just kept going off and the ... *Ping! Ping,* of the close hits are happening every three or four seconds. God! What a terrible mess we are in.

Bravo 3 had water coming in from a crack in the hull behind some of the mechanisms that run the electrical system. The pumps in the hole cannot handle the amount of water coming in and we need to use the P-250 emergency pumps to get the water out of the hole before anything drastic happens. We go to hook up the P-250's and find there is no gas to run them, the gas is all gone and we are helpless. The water keeps coming in, getting higher and higher. The water then ruptures a steam line and the 600-PSI comes into play again. I offer to try to find the leak and Leroy tells me to forget it, because there can be no repair with the water coming in until we can operate the P-250's to pump the water out.

I yell down in the hole to tell everyone not to move and I will come down to help evacuate them. As far as I am concerned no matter what Leroy has to say, the guys must get out of the hole, then in a blink of the eye, everything goes bad. Pajaro walks right in front of the steam leak and was cut right in half by the steam. I scream down into the hole ... Pajaro! Pajaro! Pajaro! I am hysterical, one of my best friends on the entire ship and now he is cut into two pieces. The other men in the gear locker put their arms around me and pull me away from the hole in the deck. They seem afraid I will go down into that terrible mess. I begin to cry a little, knowing I am a wreck and cannot take it. There is a lot of damage and we can only make six knots while we are evacuating the combat zone. Man, oh man! This old beast is in really wicked shape.

More hell breaks loose! The starboard shaft freezes up and will not turn. Minor problems have caused the ship to have limited power, but this is a major one. The shaft is really stuck and we dare not engage it for fear of further damage. The port shaft can only manage about six knots and it is like being "Dead in the Water". We are told to evacuate the area and get the hell out of the compartment. A destroyer's main defense is its movement in the water, so the enemy is unable to get a fix on you as the ship moves in a zigzag pattern. We are now totally defenseless.

We return to the locker after shoring up the mattresses and the smoking lamp was lit, signaling we were allowed to have a cigarette break. All of the smokers light up and cherish the nicotine. Some *wise ass* makes the comment, "Don't you know that those things will kill you?"

We have been at General Quarters now for about eight hours and it is taking its toll. We unwrap the provisions we have on hand and they are WWII vintage survival rations, dated 1945. We eat wieners, canned ham and crackers from the old packages. We wonder if they are still good. They also have packs of Lucky Strike cigarettes with ten in a pack.

There are cruisers, battleships and aircraft carriers. All are out of range and not near any mines. B52's fly overhead. The battleships and the cruisers keep making bombing runs and shelling, then cooling down the barrels with hoses. It was pandemonium. We all knew everything would be front-page news in the states and possibly worldwide.

We will have to go to Subic Bay again for repairs, and we are looking forward to having some fun on our runs to the bars and the EM Club. The Yardbirds (Filipino shipyard workers) will do all the work, due to a Navy contract and our ship's crew will be more or less working on planned maintenance and other minor repairs.

The ship steams to Subic at about eight knots, which is all the speed we can muster with only one shaft. The trip takes a long time. We are all worried, because we fear we will not make it before the ship falls apart. More than half the crew goes to sickbay during the trip complaining of fatigue, blurry eyes and other strange symptoms.

The Doc determines we all have scurvy and prescribes each one of us one thousand milligrams of vitamin C tablets. He calls over to a nearby hospital ship to see if they have any and sure enough, they do. How the hell can we have scurvy, nobody knows, we just take our tablets and deal with it.

The ship finally pulls into Subic Bay and there will be a lot of partying going on in the next few weeks. *Scuttlebutt* has it that the push to end the war will be enough for the Peace Treaty to finally be signed. We will certainly be the first to know. Rumors are spreading about when the war ends, everybody will get to go to Taiwan and back to Hong Kong. I sure like the idea and hope this is all over soon.

Leroy has to go to the hospital for a heart condition when we get to shore and thinks they will make him quit the Navy and get out early. All he wants is his retirement after being in for fifteen years. Leroy holds us together and helps us out with many things and knows quite a lot about everything. We are all very sad about Leroy, but we still take advantage of being back in the Ologapo City area. I decide to go to the hospital with him. I ask for permission to leave the ship and accompany him. I get permission and I feel good about going along with him.

I chat with Leroy on our way to the hospital.

"Hey Leroy a heart condition does not just come on overnight. How long do they think you have had the problem?"

"The problem is Nardone they are unable to tell whether or not there is a problem. I have to take some more tests."

"Well, Leroy, I feel better knowing the doctors only think there may be a problem."

"Nardone, I have to tell you something and promise me you will not tell a single soul."

"Leroy, if you want me to keep my mouth shut, I certainly can do that."

"You remember when we burned the holes in the side of the ship. Well, I checked out the official reports and it states that the hull is supposed to be one inch thick there. I also discovered the Captain's brother-in-law is in charge of the detail at Charleston Harbor that performs the testing and I smell a rat with the whole thing. This ship is not even seaworthy as far as I can tell and here we are sent into combat. I think the Captain is in cahoots with his brother-in-law over the whole thing."

"Leroy this is a serious accusation and I do not know what to say."

"Nardone, do you remember when Arroyo told you about the numbers not matching with the fuel we were supposed to have taken on?"

"Hey Leroy, I definitely remember when he told me and I relayed this to you in the strictest confidence."

"I think the Captain is behind the fuel discrepancy and also responsible for some of the crew having scurvy from not having enough fresh fruits and vegetables aboard."

"This is why we have scurvy, Leroy?"

"Yes, Nardone, the numbers in the record do not match either. The record shows we have taken on more fresh food than we actually have."

"I have a plan of action, Nardone. I do not need anyone to know about this. I trust you more than anybody else on the ship and that is that Nardone."

Leroy and I arrive at the hospital for his testing and I stay in the waiting room for him to finish. After the tests we head back to the ship and have another chat.

"Well Nardone, the testing is over and they say everything is okay and normal."

"That's great Leroy, I do not know what I would do without you."

"You know Nardone, there is scuttlebutt about another Operation Linebacker, oddly enough called - Linebacker II."

"I do not believe *scuttlebutt*, Leroy, why would we go do it again, why don't they just sign the Peace Treaty?"

"They are just playing games and extending the war for their own purposes. I think they will never sign."

We arrive at the ship and say our goodbyes. Leroy goes off somewhere where he does not want me to go. Back in the HT shop, I check on how the work is coming along and how the *Yardbirds* are doing. Bobo tells me they will be done in two days and we may be ready for some "R and R" somewhere.

7 RETURN TO CHARLESTON

A couple of days later, the ship does go to Hong Kong for some Rest and Relaxation, after all the repairs are done and over. We pull out of Hong Kong for the trip to Taiwan on January 23rd. All is well with Leroy's health and maybe we will not go back to the combat zone. Leroy is from a dirt-poor town and a very poor family. He was just at the height limit and was too short to get into the Navy. His family devised a device that would stretch him out and increase his height. I did not believe it at first, but Leroy was vehement about it and said that if you were not poor as shit you would not know what to do either.

On our way to Taiwan the news is passed over the 1MC.

"Men, the peace accords have been signed in Paris, officially the war is over."

The peace treaty was signed on January 27 1973. The ship may have to return to Vietnam, but it will not be under wartime conditions. We are down in the sleeping compartment, when we hear the news. Jack Kelly kisses Bobo right on the lips and the rest of us wonder if they normally did this, but we all know better. They are just caught up in the moment. We jump and yell grabbing our friends like little kids as we chant, the dirty "B" brought the commies to their knees, just like the Brits in the bar had sung for us. We start to sing other songs. Shit hits the fan and someone gets a can of shaving cream and sprays it all over another Sailor. He yells for everyone to get out the shaving cream and take no prisoners.

Everybody is ass-grabbing and creaming everybody. We pull Leroy's pants down and fill his boxer shorts with cream. Sailors come down the ladder and we just cream them like no tomorrow. We wrestle and play and sing the Wizard of Oz song, "Ding, Dong, the Wicked Witch is Dead". The engineering officer comes down the ladder shouting some commands to stop all the chaos and he gets his too. Nobody is safe from our joy and happiness.

Some of the crew are so happy about not going back to war. Men are crying with joy and their eyes glisten. It is like a scene from a movie. I take out the picture of my high school sweetheart kissing it over and over again talking about getting the real thing from my real babe.

We are on the way to Taiwan for the first peaceful Vietnamese New Year's celebration of Tet in thirteen years and the Taiwanese will be happy, but they will miss all the Sailors business. The old salts tell us the celebration will be great. Finally, the ship arrives in Taiwan harbor on the twenty-ninth of January.

Streaked across the faces of the men at the "Sea Dragon Club" (Enlisted Men's Club) is a look of joy. There is a group singing, jumping on chairs and clapping in time to the music, then "Homeward Bound" plays on the jukebox and it overwhelms me, all those Sailors humming and singing to the song. I have never been as deeply wrought with feelings as I am at this joyous period in time. This scene stays with me and I relive the moment every time I hear the song.

Taiwan is as crowded as Hong Kong. I spend the entire day sitting on a balcony, all bandaged up from a fall on the ship, watching the Tet celebrations. Dragons in the street and all types of dancers. Everything you would expect in a parade, it was a very foreign sight. The booze is good and they have Jack Daniels, but alas, I fall in love again instantly. Her name is Maria, she speaks fluent English and feels sorry for me. After being hustled by some cheap broad, Maria butts in, taking me into a room to relax and watch more of the Tet celebration. She gives me a massage and bathes me in a bubble bath. The war zone melts away as she comforts and soothes me, although I cannot forget Pajaro. His death still haunts me to this day, maybe I could have saved him. What if I had gone down in the hole? It still was one of the best drunken times I have ever had.

Maria works all night and her father is an English professor at a local college. There is a midnight curfew just like in the Philippine's and she can only come around just before midnight. Every street going out to the pier is guarded. We are anchored in the harbor and I do not remember why we did not pull up to the pier.

I have been reading articles from the "New York Times" newspaper about the war, the peace treaty and what has been happening for the last fourteen years in Vietnam. Reading brings back memories of Mr. Szabo, a Hungarian, who was a teacher from my high school and in the yearbook, he is holding a sign with "FIGHT COMMUNISM" on it. Mr. Szabo had escaped Hungary during the Soviet invasion and is a vehement anti-communist. He has seen first-hand the Communists taking over in Hungary before the invasion. Other pictures show him supporting the war in Vietnam and the scene is certainly different from all those protesters on the pier when we left Charleston, South Carolina. I think of him often.

The people of Taiwan are vehemently anti-communist also. The Taiwanese did not mind military people keeping the law and all the other things that went on. They just knew they did not want Communism. Who are the Communists anyway? I also did not like them and did not care how many of our shells killed them.

On my nineteenth birthday my draft number for the lottery was nineteen. Luckily, I enlisted in the Navy before I was drafted. They might still send in troops to evacuate the country. I try to explain the draft to

Maria, she seems to understand. All able-bodied men in Taiwan are obligated to serve two years in the military. With the peace treaty being signed, Maria and her family are afraid the whole country will face the wrath of the Communists and they will have no place to go. Her father has been trying to get into the United States for years and does not stand a chance of getting in.

My life has changed in so many ways, with many new friends and experiences. Leroy used to say, *there are men and there are morons and no in between.* Sometimes, I feel like a moron for having enlisted in the Navy before being drafted, thinking I would not have to go to war if I enlisted.

The ship leaves Taiwan on a rainy and foggy day, seems like a scene from a movie again.

I almost miss the ship's departure, and luckily, I make it in time. I have received enough non-judicial punishments and do not need an AWOL. Another beautiful port and everyone had enjoyed the Tet celebrations. The war is over and this is a blessing.

The quarterdeck officer wants to know how I got back to the ship after curfew. I pull up my pants and tell him I had been robbed, they took all my money and they also wanted my shoes. I gave them up and that is how it all happened. The whole quarterdeck crew just laughed at me and so did I. I just laughed at myself for missing the last junk before curfew. I am sure it was not this bad in the Philippines.

Back in The HT shop, I talk with Mengel and Newman and bring up the forbidden subject of the terrible shape the ship was in. We have steamed toward Hong Kong and Taiwan with mattresses holding water out and pumps running constantly.

The ship will have repairs in Subic Bay and the Yardbirds will come aboard and do their magic. We talk of how happy we will be to get back to Subic and no more war to go back to.

Illustration 6: Unknown Gunner's Mate

Dennis is worried about George, a Gunner's Mate who ran the fire control bubble in the war zone.

"I think he must be crazed by now, Dennis."

"That is what I mean, you, asshole Nardone! They took George off the ship in a straightjacket and he was doing some weird drugs he had picked up in Subic Bay before we left for Haiphong."

"What the hell are you talking about Dennis?"

"Like I said, Nardone, they took him away in a straightjacket!"

"You had liberty, but I had duty and watched the whole thing. He was a lunatic, ranting and raving about all type of foolish crap. He yelled and screamed then they shoved a needle in him and took him away."

"Jesus, what the hell happened Dennis?"

"He just cracked Nardone. He went off the deep end and they took him away."

"It could happen to anyone in the crew, but George had the fire control duty and I think it drove him crazy."

"But Dennis, George was such a nice guy and he always had time to smoke a joint with you whenever he had some weed.

"Big deal Nardone!"

"Well I will miss him and he ain't in no body bag, but he might as well be dead. I feel sorry for his wife."

"I had no idea he was married, Dennis."

"We all know the war is over, but all of us might go off the deep end someday, it just may take longer to catch up to you."

"There you go again, *Mr. Psychology*."

"It's true, Nardone, the stress may catch up to us."

Bob sits and listens. He and I both knew George and Dennis are really close and tight. They hung out together and rode motorcycles together back in Charleston.

The next day at General Quarters there is a moment of silence for George and we are all told about what had happened. Everyone has a strained look on their face, there is still that long trip home wanting to get back to the USA.

Leroy finds another spot in the hull to be welded and he has me cut the plate for it and just like before we burn a hole right in the side of the ship. Leroy leaves to get the previous x-ray tests to look at them again. He comes back and does not have the results. They were nowhere to be found aboard or at the Charleston Navy Base.

"What the hell are we going to do Leroy, there is water coming in?"

"The bilge pumps should take care of it for now, Nardone."

"The leak is not that bad and it is right at the waterline."

"What do you want me to do Leroy?"

"Go somewhere and stay out of trouble. I have other things to do right now."

We have our favorite places to skate work and I go to one of mine and take a nap. I tell Sanchez where I will be if he needs to come and get me.

The next day we try a monumental task. Leroy receives a fax from main control in Charleston and in the report the section of the ship we are working on is one inch thick, just like the other section of the ship we patched before. He decides to weld it from the outside and he goes over in a Bosun's chair, a device used to suspend a person from a rope to work aloft.

The engineers manipulate water in compartments to list the ship as much to port as possible and Leroy uses magnets to hold up a plate from one crossbeam to the next. I wonder why we did not just use a mattress and some plywood. A breaker is set up and we can shut off the juice when the waves get high. The sea is extremely calm and there are hardly any waves to speak of. Leroy welds the plate right where it needs to be and the water stops coming in when they straighten out the ship from the list to Port.

The Captain passes the word over the 1MC about Leroy's accomplishment and bravery. We all thought that he should be commended. Leroy loved the attention. He is definitely proud of himself, as well he should be. He could have been electrocuted or washed away by the waves, but fortunately the seas were calm.

Even though "R and R" is great, we all want to get home and that is that. There has been some talk among the officers about taking the Atlantic route back to Charleston to circumnavigate the globe, which would be a very long trip. The engineering officer is stuck between a rock and a hard place. He wants to make the Atlantic trip really bad and see some different parts of the world, but he is stuck with the price of fuel oil, and who we would buy it from. This made the difference between routes.

So, the decision is made to go home via the Pacific, which is actually the shorter route. Things are hot in the Middle East right now and we might have a problem using the Suez Canal. The Quartermasters have to calculate mileage, fuel consumption and many other factors. We take the same route back home because of the problems with the   purchase of fuel oil, just more politics!

When the trip is canceled, Leroy and I talk one night about how many places he had been in the Navy. One time in Africa, when the ship pulled into Cape Town, he couldn't even leave the ship. He was pissed off remembering being in South Africa and said it sucked fighting a war, when you are considered half a citizen back in the states and that South Africa sucked rocks.

The conversation made him solemn and he starts to tell me about what he found in the hulls x-ray reports.

"Nardone these reports are all screwed up and there is nothing I can do except tell the proper authorities and hope for the best."

"Well, go tell the Captain, Leroy. He can take care of it."

"Nardone, he just may be the cause of all the problems we are having. I cannot go to him and I have to figure out what to do."

"Well, go to the Engineering Officer. He should be able to help out in some way."

"I have to tell the proper people, Nardone, and it ain't the Engineering Officer. I am burning up inside after all my years in the Navy. The only thing we have is trust and we may have lost that. I cannot stand it any longer. I do not want to tell you anymore Nardone."

"You are not telling me anything anyway. Leroy, you just got to do what you got to do, and leave me out of it."

"I will leave you out of it, Nardone, but it will not help me. I have to keep it to myself and do not mention this conversation to anybody, not to anyone!"

"You can trust me, Leroy. I will not speak a word about whatever it is that you are not telling me anyway."

Leroy blurts out something about the rotten bastard and what a mean son of a bitch he is and stomps away.

I talk about the whole thing with Sanchez, even though I promised Leroy not say anything to anybody. All Mike had to say is *scuttlebutt* will fly. We will all hear something soon enough.

I go up to the fo'c'sle to relax and watch my friends the dolphins play after working all day and sort out what Leroy has told me. I still have to stand a forty-eight-hour rotation on sounding and security watch. All the men in the Hull Technician's shop stand these watches.

I think about my Uncle Mike who is my age and also in the Navy. He marries a Filipino while in Subic Bay. The Captain and the ship's Chaplin perform the ceremony. I wonder if she is a hooker or a student or what, but he never writes to me about these things. He seems to be very happy.

News comes while we are at a chow line get-together. Words fly up and down. Men are leaving the chow line to talk to friends who might know more about the *scuttlebutt*. The word is the Captain is in deep shit! The XO (Executive Officer) will take over the ship and relieve the Captain of his command. Nobody knew the circumstances, but the same *scuttlebutt* came from everywhere and every possible concept came up and nobody knew what to think.

The crew hopes the Captain is in some real trouble, because we are all bitter and hate him. He loves to mete out punishment at Captain's Mast and screw everybody. He is known as one of the worst in the Fleet. We discuss shipmate Oalmans stiff sentence, including reduction in rank and thirty days extra duty, and a $300.00 fine, all for having a pet squirrel in a cage. Yet, the Captain gives a black man only a thirty-day confinement to the ship for having a loaded gun aboard, due to his fear. The Captain seems to relish the discipline he dispenses, but there seems to be something not right with him.

Leroy decides to seek out the mess cooks for more information, because they cook for the officers and hear it all, they will certainly know what is happening. Mess cooks know everything and are loose-tongued. Leroy tells us to go back to the HT shop. Many men are hovering around the entry hatch and Sanchez bitches about the cigarette smoke. The shop is also full of men from The Repair Division. Bobo is the most incessant talker. He really hates the Captain and has been given some stiff punishments.

"I hope he gets what he deserves for whatever he did."

Bobo is sitting there like a little forlorn boy, all he wants to do is get promoted and get off of the ship. He continues on a rant.

"I do not care what they do to him, all I want to do is get out of here and get back home!"

Leroy comes back to the shop.

"Men, the Captain has been placed under arrest this morning and he is confined to his cabin. The circumstances are unclear, but it has something to do with the ship's readiness reports, and the fact that his Brother-In-Law is in charge of COMDESRON SIX back in Charleston. My feelings are the ship should not even be rated as seaworthy. I think he got us into the war zone for his own purposes to obtain a promotion to Commodore."

"There has been an investigation going on over the phones, the 1MC and also back in the states. I am the one who uncovered the whole thing. I did not know what to do at first, because I was unsure of who may have been in on it. I radioed back to the states for the NIS to investigate and this is what has led to the Captain being arrested."

Leroy tells us more.

"There are problems with all facets of the readiness reports and everything from the hull to the compressors is out of whack. If the reports showed the ships real condition, we would never have left the port for Vietnam."

There is no response from anybody and nobody knew what to do. The plot has been uncovered. There is a special Quarters for Muster and Inspection in twenty minutes to inform the crew about everything.

I am mumbling and grumbling, while beating a metal bar on the workbench. Bobo and I talk about how we hope someone will kill the bastard. We are just trying to figure out what has gone on. Leroy hopes the Navy does not send the motherfucker off to do desk duty for the rest of his career, which they would do, rather than get the bad press.

Leroy comments.

"I hope they give him what he has coming to him and they do not try to cover it up. They should give all the negative press to him and not the ship."

Naturally, we chatted about the fact that if the captain fucks up they will slap his pee-pee and give him some minor shit to deal with. If we do minor things we get slapped with major punishments. The Captain just loved to be a sadistic son of a bitch at Captain's Mast and mete out stiff punishments.

The whistle blows, and the announcement is heard over the 1 MC.

"All hands report for Quarters for Muster and Inspection."

The "R" division gathers in its normal spot on the fantail and musters up. Anger and strain are etched on all the faces of the men. Stearns, with his wrinkled and sea-worn bearded face, growls as he speaks of all the breakdowns the ship has been through. He, Mengel, and I are talking about losing the steering, dropping the load and other failures of the ship, including denying the HT shop permission to have a coffee pot and taking away the one we have for no good reason.

The Captain made past announcements so smooth, such as, *Wear your dog tags, telling us to do a good job, hit the NVA, and be strong.*

The Chief's and the Officers appear from their special meeting and come to the fantail. They announce for us to go to attention at ease, which means to pay attention and listen to what they are about to say.

The Engineering Officer reads the prepared statement in the angriest of tones, tempered with officialese. He looks as if he could burst, you could just tell and he begins to read slowly.

"Men there has been a lot of hot scuttlebutt over the last few days and I know everyone is feeling tense. The situation is this, there have been some misleading statements on official documents and no one is quite sure of the circumstances. We do know the Captain is at the core of these problems and that is that. Nothing can be proven for right now. Due to the gravity of the situation the captain is being placed under arrest for his own protection and the XO will be taking over command of the ship. There will be an armed guard on the Captain's sea cabin and you are not to communicate with the guards or bother them in any way. They are not allowed to speak while on duty and that is that. The duration of this situation will be until we enter Charleston Harbor and dock."

"The men standing *Sounding and Security Watch,* who rotate to the bridge every hour, are not allowed to communicate with the guard, as this will only make the situation worse and the *scuttlebutt* will fly. You are not to write home about the situation and there is a chance that mail may be censored or discontinued completely until we hit port. Anything that is communicated may keep justice from being done and that is that. Normally I would ask for questions, but not in this situation. This is all for now and you are all dismissed and the normal work schedule will commence in a half an hour."

Mengel, and I start up a conversation about how they might not punish the Captain and what he actually did anyway.

"I think that he is just being arrested and it is just crap for his own protection. We are not going to hurt him, or are we?"

"I am sure that we have the capacity to hurt the bastard. He did something and he will pay the price is the way that I feel about it."

"There is no deeper anger than that of being betrayed when you trust someone and he ends up being arrested."

"If we were in the jungle someone would probably have shot him a long time ago and that would be that. I have heard that that happens in the Nam all the time."

Dennis and I start to laugh even if it seems strange to laugh, but I guess it is a normal reaction under stress. We just keep laughing uncontrollably and do not know why. There seems to be no choice but to make jokes about everything and just go back to work.

Dennis and I continue talking about how angry everyone seemed to be and how our bonds had become stronger. We have stuck together and helped each other and been "Tin Can Tight".

Here is this monster of a man and he is all locked up. Fate has caught him by the balls and that is that. As we steam home I pass by the guards and the Captain's cabin many times as I stand watch. I do my diligent best and do not speak to the Sailors standing guard over the man that was in charge of this entire ship. I only write about it once in my diary.

The fear oozes out of the cracks around the door to the cabin. I can see him, behind that gray door, unable to sleep or eat. I can feel him sweating and pacing the deck.

Then my thoughts turn to what a cold-hearted bastard he is. An evil son of a bitch! We all want to kill him by poisoning his food, but the Master-at-Arms oversees the preparation of his meals and is in charge of delivering them.

The looks we exchange as I stand my watch makes me realize that the guards are really afraid of a Sailor trying to get at the captain, they even talk of pulling a "CRAZY" and blowing him away themselves. The Captain just wanted to get promoted all this time and here he is under arrest. Leroy stays away from this entire part of the ship. He does not want anything to do with the man or his sea cabin arrest. I feel there are things Leroy is not telling us. I think he knows much more, than he is letting on.

The XO must have relished the thought of taking charge. I mean here he was in charge of the ship and was promoted due to the circumstances. I wonder if he even cared about the man who he was one step below on the chain of command. The Captain became a casualty of his own madness and the next in charge took over. This is the way it was.

Oh! The hell we have been through. The "Operation Linebacker" operations and the NGFS down south. We have gone in and out of the war zone and fought our own individual wars. Stearns re-enlists while in the war zone and collects a $10,000 tax-free bonus. We do not have to pay taxes while in the war zone and isn't this just great. There is a little ceremony for Stearns and the entire "R" division attends. We all congratulate him on his new lifestyle. He has only been in for six years and now he will have to do ten more years. You really have to do it this way and some guys have no choice but to re-enlist. There is no other life for them and they will be able to retire when they have served their twenty years.

We are all heroes. The men who were half dehydrated in those one-hundred-degree boiler rooms with the sounds of the boiler so loud and the cotton plugged into their ears. Barely feeling the rumbles, and the *Thud! Thud!* Of the cannons going off. Engel tells me that it feels like *she* belches and you are in her stomach. Everybody talks of the ship as a *she* as if *she* is alive. *She* fires her guns, and *she* blows her stack. When we had passed by the Arizona Memorial, we all had said that the Sailors went down with *her*. We are the corpuscles in the blood stream, as the men will say. We have painted her decks and cooled down her barrels. She was a *she* and it was the sea and *she*.

While in Hong Kong, the gutless Chief Petty Officer who was supposed to know what to do, made me do something and I refuse to do it until the Engineering Officer approves it. The used-up OBA (Oxygen Breathing Apparatus) canisters are supposed to be disposed of in thirty-gallon drums or you could use a garbage can filled with fresh water. Well anyway, the Chief made me put them in little pails of water and I wondered if he had ever been to school or done this before. The water turns into hydrochloric acid and will eat all the paint off the fantail. I call the Engineering Officer and tell him what I think should be done and I am sure glad I did. The Engineering Officer tells me to do what the Chief wants me to do and if anything happens, he would put the blame on him. I just watch as the little buckets overflow and eat all the paint off of the fantail.

I am very happy when the Chief is written up and it is placed in his records, to show he did not have sufficient experience to give commands about things he knew nothing about.

Mike Sanchez had an opinion that the Chief is the one who placed the wrench in the right place as an act of sabotage, before we ever left for the war.

I ask.

"What makes you think that Mike?"

"I just have my feelings about it, someone else confessed and got out of going into the war zone and went to the brig instead."

"So, it is just a feeling that you have and you do not have any evidence?"

"No, I do not have anything except an opinion, Nardone. I do remember the chief wanted to know where we kept all the different tools and that was unusual because Chief's don't usually want to know where we keep the tools.

On the way to Hawaii, I am chosen to lead a group of men from the Engineering Division on a special detail. There are many fifty-gallon drums stored on the *helo* deck. We had no idea what is stored in them, but think it might be Agent Orange, which had previously been banned in-country while we were there. The barrels had orange stripes on them with no other markings. We are given the job of disposing of it and washing it over the side of the ship.

There is no special clothing, so I bitch about needing protective clothing. The only protection we are given is rubber gloves. We start to hack the barrels open with hatches and roll the barrels on their side, dumping it overboard. The stuff spills all over us as we try to remain sane and wonder what we are actually handling. We are also told to make sure we use the hatchets on the barrels or they will float. Jack Kelly gets really disgusted about the whole thing and wants to stop the entire process. Complaining to the Engineering Officer does him no good and we are told to follow orders to get rid of the stuff and heave the barrels over the side after emptying them.

So, we dump the crap into the ocean, the Captain has been arrested and here the crew is doing what we are told again. It reminds me of the huge island of garbage I saw on the way to the war zone, as we pollute the world some more. I am disturbed by the idea that we are still sailing with mattress patches in place without pulling in for repair after Operation Linebacker.

On our way to Hawaii a telegram is sent to the ship for Sanchez informing him his wife has had a baby boy. We are basically a floating city and could receive telegrams from home while at sea.

A couple of days in Pearl Harbor and then we leave for Panama. Meaning we will spend another two weeks at sea with nothing for entertainment, except card games and the nightly movie.

On the way to Panama, Arroyo tells me we may have to endure another storm and I am not ready for this. We are up night and day as usual. I am standing *Sounding and Security Watches* every eighteen hours and watching the guys standing the *Mids*. I have to wake up at 2330 at night. Most guys do not sleep before they stand the mid- watch and hardly get any rest at all. No wonder we drink gallons and gallons of coffee. The forty-eight-day trip back to the real world is hard to endure. Men get their rest when they can and take what we call *nooners,* sleeping on top of the lockers with a pillow from our rack. We get an hour and a half for lunch break and I think they plan it this way so you can get some sleep.

I still cannot get over the fact that we all have had scurvy due to a lack of vitamin C. My back hurts most of the time after having fallen down a ladder while moving ammo and holding onto a five-inch shell, so I report to sick bay many times. The doc sends me for x-rays at Pearl Harbor, and the results show damage to my lumbar region near T10 and T 11 vertebra.

My back problems do not bother me too much and I begin to think about all the problems the ship is still having. The boilers have "salted up", meaning contaminated with salt water and we have to go on emergency power. The ship has dropped the load more than five times. All I want is a pier, to be home and have a nice place to sleep for a long time. Checking into a motel for a few days when we get back will be a sweet treat.

Letters came from home. My father's and step-mother's prayers for peace have been answered, they declare. I did not feel peaceful though. The ship is a constant source of fear, thinking something might start on fire or blow up, and fearing I would have to use the broom routine again on a steam leak.

We are finally nearing Panama after days at sea and have a nice trip through the canal, stopping on both sides again. Everyone is counting the days now it will not be too long. Many men mingle all night, unable to sleep and talk about having made it. The men talk about what happened to Pajaro and George, the Gunner's Mate. Feeling joy about the final trip home, not the war was a contributing factor to the sleeplessness. Everyone is smiling, joking and telling stories of the times we have had on our trip to the war and the eventual signing of the Peace Treaty. We don't look as solemn and zombie like anymore. We all talk of running down the gangway and kissing the pier.

It is a sweltering day and the ship docks on the east side of the canal. The day we are to leave the whistle blows at 0500, an ungodly hour.

Uniformed men come aboard stomping around and making everybody get dressed and report to Quarters. We are all talking about how something bad must have happened and have no clue what is going on. We are not allowed to use our lockers and many men have to go to Quarters in their skivvies with no socks.

"Maybe war has broken out with Panama!" Riccobono chuckles.

As the sun comes up, everyone is rushed onto the deck quickly. Vans pull up and the scene becomes obvious to everyone. Men with pistols strapped to them come aboard. They are from the NIS (Naval Investigative Service). Dogs are also unloaded from the vans. The deck is hot, making it tough to stand still. The dogs go all over the ship and inspect every locker with an NIS officer present. I think to myself, *who would be so stupid as to keep a stash of drugs in their locker*? I am in disbelief when they take a couple of men away in handcuffs.

We are standing for hours and some of us demand to get our shower shoes, because of the hot deck. Leroy comments that anyone stupid enough to do drugs deserves to be thrown out of the Navy and given a BCD (Bad Conduct Discharge). Many hours later, the handcuffed men are finally taken away, and we are able to return to our normal routine. We all continue on as if nothing has happened and stand around in the Hull Tech's shop talking about the Sailors who are taken off the ship.

The Captain is allowed out of his cabin with guards for some exercise on the pier. The Marines guard him now instead of the Sailors from our ship. The *scuttlebutt* still flies about what he has done to be arrested. The crew is still pissed off about the whole thing. The same thought comes to me that we are all actually in a prison aboard this old beast of a ship. We just want to get back to the United States.

We have to travel through the "Devil's Triangle" again. Most of the crew has read the paperback about the triangle which has been passed around. On the way to Nam we went through this area and look at what has happened to us since.

The nights are very calm. The sunrises and sunsets are spectacular. We hit a plankton deposit one night and I did not know what the hell it was. Barber who is an old salt explains to me how the plankton die all at once and the chemical reaction in their bodies gives off a neon like glow. Seeing all those billions of plankton glowing and being churned up by the ship is one hell of a sight. I watch the scene and I am mesmerized for hours as the full moon reflects ominously on the water.

I decide to go to the bridge and shoot the breeze with Peter Arroyo, a Puerto Rican from New York City who tells wild stories about his gangland father and his upbringing. We have a good friendship and I speak Spanish with him and he tries to teach me more. We often talk about prejudice and how rampant it is aboard the ship. The close quarters on the ship, gives the crew no choice but to try and get along. I think many men left most of their prejudice back in the war zone. He takes out some charts to show me where we have been.

"Nardone we have traveled about fifty thousand miles on this trip and it sure uses one hell of a lot of fuel. The ship burns about one gallon for every half a mile we go."

"Peter, please don't tell me how far we have traveled, all I know is that in two days we will be back at Charleston Pier and the food from my favorite restaurant will sure taste good."

"Nardone, home for me is New York City, and I will be happy to get there."

"You do realize half the crew has to stay aboard the ship while the rest of the crew gets two weeks of leave. Which section are you in Peter?"

"I have duty with the first section and have to stay aboard for the whole two weeks.

"Peter, I cannot think of anything to tell you."

"Nardone, all I feel like doing is holding my Mama and crying and I probably will for the whole two weeks."

"How about you Nardone, what section do you have?"

"I have leave for the first section and that sure as hell will be nice. When I get back from leave, I will be on a four by eight rotation since I have been approved for sounding and security watch."

"I bet you saw a lot up here being on the bridge when we were in the war zone."

"I saw the whole thing Nardone, the whole damned thing every minute of it. I just felt terrible when they took George away in a straight-jacket and I watched as they stuck the needle in his leg."

"Soon we will be home and you will get the chance to do exactly that Peter."

"I still have to wait two weeks you, bastard, I have to stay here when we get to Charleston."

'Well I gotta go watch another sunset Peter and enjoy the view, then it is time to hit the rack. The war is over now and we had a part in ending it."

"See ya later, Nardone."

We are a very tight crew and everybody knows almost everyone else. Standing watch and going all over the ship allowed me to know many of the men. Whether it was from an accident with the 600-PSI steam or a straightjacket you could still feel what the in-country guys must have felt like when they took casualties.

The ship left Charleston about one hundred and fifty days ago. We went all together and all together we are returning to the states, unlike the in-country troops which are rotated in and out.

I talk with Arroyo again later.

"Hey Peter, I remember in the war zone on one of the trips back to Subic Bay, you said we were short on fuel and might have to take a storm head on. What was the exact problem and what do you remember?"

Peter recants his story.

"Oh Nardone, what am I supposed to tell you. I have no memory of what happened and I do not know what I may have said."

"Sounds to me Peter like you are afraid to tell me something and get involved or maybe you got involved and do not want me to know."
"You are nuts Nardone, me get involved in some type of thievery of the fuel or something?"

"That might not be the case but I remember you passing me the note and the talk we had about the difference in the amount of fuel shown on the books and what we actually took on, and that is no laughing matter Peter."

I sighed and wondered what to do since I was intrigued with all the stuff that had happened and the Captain's arrest.

"You know Arroyo, the Captain has been arrested and there is a lot of funny crap that has gone on. When we all had scurvy, did you know the Doc discovered the official requisition records showed we were bringing on more fresh fruit and vegetables than we actually were.

Peter turned away and did not seem to want to talk about it and I wondered if it was because he was afraid about what might happen to him if he mentioned anything to anyone in his division.

"Peter are you scared about something?"

'You are dammed right! I am afraid about all of it Nardone!"

"Is there something that you are not telling me Arroyo?"

"I guess I can trust you, Nardone."

"I certainly hope that you feel that way Arroyo."

"One of the Puerto Ricans, who works the officers mess deck has a big set of ears and he overheard facts about a big investigation going on with the ship and everything it has been involved in, not just the arrest of the Captain. There was mention of the black Market and what a huge case it was for the NIS to handle. The NIS had also brought in Interpol and the German Secret Police."

"I had no idea the Germans even had secret police."

"That is just the name of the unit, Nardone you know they are like the FBI or something like that."

"Well Arroyo, I will just have to keep my mouth shut and not say anything to anybody and hope to make it home and everything is okay and we do not get restricted to the ship or some crazy shit like that."

"I just want to pull up to the pier and get on the phone."

"You got any idea how long that the line is going to be at the only phone booth on the pier, Peter?"

"I hear that they are going to time the phone calls and have the Master-at-Arms of the Navy base by the phone booth."

"Well I can say a lot in a few short minutes."

I look for Leroy to verify what Arroyo said about the black market crap and I am sure Leroy will know something. I scour the ship and ask everyone if they have seen Sass. I finally find him and Bobo getting ready to do some work.

"Hey there Leroy, you got a few minutes to talk about something really important. Can we chat out on the fantail right near where you are going to be working?"

"Yeah Nardone, I got a few minutes. Is it something related to race relations?"

"No, No Leroy, not at all, now let's just go and get this over with."

No one else was around as we walked toward the fantail.

"I just talked to Arroyo and he told me that the Puerto Ricans working the officer's mess have heard some shit about the black market and the ship and the Captain. What the hell is going on Leroy?"

Leroy let out a sigh saying he could not tell me very much and that was basically nothing.

"There is nothing appropriate to tell you Nardone. It does not have anything to do with trust. I am unable to tell anyone what is going on and that is that!"

"Come on Leroy, you can trust me."

At this point Leroy gets very serious and tells me to treat him as a superior in rank.

"I am your superior and that is that, Nardone. I am not at liberty to discuss anything. I am even surprised about the *scuttlebutt* from the Officers mess."

"I really don't know what they are talking about and I really don't know nothing about nothing, Nardone. That is all there is to it. We are pulling into port in two days and that is an affirmative as far as I can tell"

I run into Arroyo again and we do not discuss anything at all except to exchange hellos and remark about how we were two hours closer to home. I go to the mess decks and grab a cup of coffee and decide to rearrange my locker for the umpteenth time.

I read a letter from home as I sit cross-legged on the deck in front of my little locker space. It is from Mom of course, who else would it be from. She writes more letters to me than anyone else and they are always the same. Relaying the news about everything and everyone, this time about a cousin who is getting married. I wish I could be there in my dress whites with my new ribbons which included, the Combat Action Medal and the Vietnam Service Medal. I did not have a good conduct medal and never would get one due to my bad attitude.

Sanchez strolls up and takes a seat on the locker tops next to mine and I assume he is going to bother me again about the duty rotation and what our friendship has meant. All that crap and he did.

"You know, Nardone, I have a new baby and I cannot even go home to be with him."

"At least it is a boy Sanchez, you could not ask for more and the two weeks will go by fast."

"It will not you fool, I want to be home with my family, and you are the only one left to swap duty time. You can have the first rotation."

"Mike you have been asking me to switch with you for two weeks now and I am the only one left to switch with. Do you think that I want to stay on this old beast for two more weeks and stand the watches and all that crap? My father and step-mother have a party planned for me and I want to be there. They planned it for the first weekend of my arrival home and that is that!"

Sanchez starts to cry and the tears flow down his cheeks. I did not know what to do. We are all so emotional at this point. He looks like a character out of a movie as he begs and pleads with me to go to the Engineering Officer to make it official and do him the biggest favor he could ask for.

"What is this crap with all the tears, Sanchez, I do not know how to handle all the emotions that you are obviously going through."

He sobs some more.

"Is this some type of act you have thought up or are you really in a crying mood?

"I am in a crying mood, Nardone."

"I thought so and you certainly look sincere."

"Just one favor, Nardone, Just one favor. I have never asked you to do anything for me before."

"Mike, Mike, Mike, just stop the crying and I will talk to the Engineering Officer tomorrow. I guess that we should have something in writing so you will have to ask one of the Personnelman that is your friend to type something up. That way we can look like we know what we are doing."

Sanchez gives me a big hug and he is still crying and acting all emotional. If it was not for Sanchez, I might have gone AWOL in Subic Bay and my life would really be different. I might as well stay aboard for two weeks more and if the request is approved, Sanchez will have to go through all the crap of asking to have his leave dates changed.

I cannot believe how much I have changed, along with my point of view. I would never have done something like this before going into the Navy.

My point of view certainly changed when I found out the ship will pull into port the night before with the Captain and release him to the Shore Patrol. He will not be seen by any of the friends, families or the press for that matter. I still wonder what the hell he did to be in his position. We pull into port and let the son of a bitch off in his manacles and chains. He sure as hell knows how to screw up your outlook on the trust factor. We have to pull back out into the harbor and wait for the right tide to pull back in the next morning. The whole thing is a strain on the crew, including me.

While I am out and about again, Sanchez and I run into each other and discuss his duty section, I tell him it would require a special chit to be signed and approved by all the right persons. He begins to cry again.

"How can I tell you what this means to me Nardone?"

"I have a very good idea how much it means to you Sancho, my old buddy, why do you think I am doing it."

"But, But, But, Nardone, I will be able to leave the ship and go home to Texas if I do not have any duty. I will be able to see my family and take my new baby son with me."

He could not stop sobbing and I wanted to go somewhere else and not watch him anymore.

"Sancho, I have to run a few errands around the ship, collect some debts and get some of my money and interest back. As you know, I can only charge ten percent which is the best rate aboard and everybody comes to me for money."

"Nardone, you know that running a slush fund is as illegal as it comes."

"I know my man but I like doing it and what will they do to me if they catch me."

"You have been in so much trouble, Nardone, I do not know how you will make it without getting a BCD and screwing up your entire life."

"It will never come to that Sanchez, and I have never seen anyone get busted for running a slush fund."

Sancho shrugged his shoulders and said.

"I remember when you got caught with the dope and the Captain gave you the sentence of three days with bread and water. Everybody fed you food while you were in the ICU compartment and you even ate more than if you would have been in the chow line."

I responded half-heartedly to his comments.

"I felt sick after just one day of bread and water, so I was happy everybody wanted to feed me. The Master at Arms followed me all over the place. He only gave me one biscuit and one glass of water for my breakfast, then he stood there and watched me eat it too."

"Sanchez, I really have to go to take care of business. We just got paid and we all need to have our money in order, besides I am tired of talking about switching leave section with you, because it is perfectly legal and can be done."

A couple of guys come over to where we are and strike up a conversation and ask what we are up to.

Sanchez tells Bobo.

"I cannot believe it Bobo, but Nardone is changing leave sections with me and I am feeling great about it.'"

Bobo responds.

"Why the hell did you do that Nardone? This means you will have to stay aboard for the first two weeks after we have pulled into Charleston."

"I know Bobo, but I just cannot bear to see Sancho have to stay aboard for those two weeks having to stay away from his wife and his new son. I only believe in doing unto others as I would have them do unto me. This is my belief."

"Nardone you certainly have changed since I met you almost a year ago. You are not a spoiled brat anymore."

"Gee, thanks Bobo! I could not ask for a better comment to make my day and now we have to deal with pulling into port after our tour of the war zone with all that has happened over the past few months."

Sanchez chimes in with a rhythmic tone.

"Well, Nardone, you did not even ask me for money to switch duty. I do not know how to thank you. I will get started on the paperwork first thing in the morning right after quarters."

"You better do it before I change my mind and you better hope that there is not a difference of opinion with our switching sections, my man. You know the higher-ups have to approve everything and they may not do it."

"Why wouldn't they do it Nardone just give me one good reason."

"I cannot think of one and I doubt anyone will argue about you being able to go home to your family after being in the war zone."

Bobo reacts excitedly.

"I am going to hit the pit and be ready for tomorrow when we pull into port."

I respond.

"How the hell can you think about sleeping at a time like this? We are pulling into Home town, USA and I am unable to stay calm."

An announcement is made we will pull into port the night before our official arrival to escort the Captain off the ship. As we pull into port that evening, the whole crew can see a Navy van with Marines standing guard at the pier.

Kelly comes over to chat.

"Scuttlebutt has it those are the guards for the Captain and it will be televised on the national news."

The Captain is escorted off the ship under armed guard and he has his hat pulled way down low, like a *Mafioso,* so the press will not be able to get a good picture of him. The Captain amazes everyone, when he adjusts his cap and performs a military salute to the colors as he preps to cross the gangway. He goes directly to the van with the Marines standing by it. He will definitely get his just punishment are my thoughts.

The ship pulls out of port after dropping of the Captain and will pull in again in the morning for our "official arrival".

I end up staying up all night long, rapping with friends and drinking loads of coffee. When sunrise comes. I have my regular breakfast of five sausages and five scrambled eggs. I remember one time, when the pain in the ass Captain had the Master at Arms watch me to make sure I ate all my breakfast and did not leave any. We are getting ready to set the sea and anchor detail to pull into port again.

We are getting really close now and we can see groups of people on the pier. There are no protesters this time and the people are mostly family members of the crew, along with other Sailors who have asked permission to welcome us back home. As we are securing the lines and butting up against the pier, we can hear everybody shouting - Welcome home! So good to see you! Many are waving flags, and the whole scene is pandemonium.

We all leave the ship and mingle with everyone on the pier. Leroy's wife gives me a big hug, and so do other wives. Everybody was just hugging and crying, and hugging and crying.

There was even a group of bar flies from one of the local clubs and they were doing their share of hugging and crying too. Imagine some guys on the ship received letters from them, and they were just a bunch of floozies from some local bar.

Eventually there is a line at the phone booth of about one hundred Sailors. Phone calls have time limits, so everyone can get to make a call home. My turn at the phone booth finally comes up after about two hours. I am home now and the conversations turn to what we are going to do with our first taste of freedom on the shores of the homeland.

My father is furious when he finds out that I will not be home for a little over two weeks. He cannot understand why I would change duty sections with someone else. He is really pissed off. Ranting and raving about the party he and my stepmother had planned. I ask him if they are able to change the dates and he just gets more upset and continues to rant. Obviously, he has no idea what my shipmates and I have been through. I start to get emotional and tell him my time is up for the phone call. I sure am glad, because I am not in the mood to talk about it anymore with an angry father.

On returning to the ship, I begin my preparations to go over to my favorite local bar, and maybe run into some of the barflies whom I had left behind many months before.

Here my journey ends about my tour in Vietnam. The ship went on another tour of South America, which is not in this account and I was discharged from the Navy in 1974.

Back to the present day and the beginning of my journey.

About five years after my discharge I started counseling at the Veterans Outreach Center, sometime in the late 1970's. I also started to rewrite my diary from the Navy based on the advice of a VA shrink that had interviewed me about eight months ago. He had said as part of therapy it would be good to try to remember the whole tour of Vietnam and I certainly remember everything as I read my diary. I go once a week and talk to a counselor named Gary Beikirch, at the Veteran's Outreach Center in Rochester, NY. Gary is a Green Beret and Medal of Honor recipient and I had one hell of a lot of respect for him.

Gary asked me when I had been in Vietnam and I said January 27, 1973 was the date that I remembered the most because that was the day the peace treaty in Paris was signed and the entire crew went a little wacky over it. I told him that I had been writing about my experiences and it seemed to take the edge off but I still could not stop the drinking and the doping all the time.

We had many conversations about many things and he helped me sign up for disability benefits with the VA from a fall that I had taken down a ladder aboard the ship during rearming. I told him that I had been recommended for a medal that was just one step short of the Navy Cross but you had to have been awarded the Good Conduct Medal in order to receive the commendation and that was one award that I sure as hell was never going to get from anybody. My records were a mess with disciplinary crap and I was a terrible Sailor, but if I was so terrible why would they recommend me for the medal in the first place?

I will utilize any and all available resources to the utmost of my abilities in order to gain the goals of my unit whatever those shall be.

I used this motto in my everyday life in how I treated everything and now I was told that I had one of the worst cases of PTSD on the roster at the Veterans Outreach Center.

When Gary told me, I did not know what to think. He put it in the best of his counselor type talks.

"Terry you are in the top ten worst cases of PTSD that we have here at the VOC. We have over two hundred clients and you make the top ten as far as severity."

"Gee, thanks Gary, what will that get me? I have filed for disability with the VA and have been told all my records are classified. I have no proof of being in combat other than my DD-214 discharge papers. They say the DD-214 is not enough proof of combat and the local VA office is even making fun of me when I call on the phone."

"The one thing I do know is that you are supposed to go through your memories and decompress. This process is supposed to be helpful."

Gary did his best to remain calm as he talks about my therapy.

"I have been rereading my diary I kept while in the Navy, and the last date is May 25 1973, some months after coming home from the war and the rest is history as they say. I have nightmares and all the symptoms. Now you are telling me I am in the top ten cases."

I sigh and keep talking.

"Do you think the seizures I am having are symptoms of PTSD?"

"Well we are pursuing that with the VA medical system and we do not know what to do. It will probably not do you any good to have them declared as part of your PTSD. It certainly will help if your records are ever declassified."

"I just want my life to be as normal as possible and get on with it, Gary."

"I do not blame you Terry. I guess all you can do is try to get a job and make a living and do the best you can."

Gary said my time was up and we would meet the same time next week. I wish I was able to have a session two times a week, it would do me some good. All I could do was hope.

I continue with healing and counseling to this day.

Illustration 7: Damage to the USS Bordelon from Russian MIG aircraft

AFTERWORD

History of the USS Bordelon (DD881)

Illustration 8: Ship's Patch with Motto

There are good ships, and there are wood ships, the ships that sail the sea. But the best ships are friendships, and may they always be. The Bordelon was a Gearing class destroyer (DD), the last class of US Navy destroyers to see combat in World War II. The Gearing class was a modification to the previous Sumner class, a modification which added fourteen feet to the length for additional fuel storage to increase the operating range for the vast areas of the Pacific. With the increased length, the Gearing class was marginally faster than the Sumner class. These destroyers were to be the mainstay of the US Navy for over twenty years. The ship was named in honor of Staff Sergeant William J. Bordelon, USMC, who was posthumously awarded the Congressional Medal of Honor for bravery during the battle of Tarawa (Gilbert Islands).The USS Bordelon was commissioned on June 5, 1945, with Cdr. Michael J Luosey USN, as her first commanding officer. Upon completion of outfitting and provisioning, Bordelon stood out from Galveston on June 22, 1945 for shakedown in the area of Guantanamo Bay, Cuba, arriving there on the 25th. Upon completion of these maneuvers she cleared the Caribbean on July 22 for Norfolk Navy Yard for post shakedown availability. In the summer of 1945 Bordelon underwent conversion to a Radar Picket Destroyer (DDR) at Norfolk Naval Shipyard. This change removed the torpedo tubes and added additional 40 mm guns. Most visible was the addition of a tripod after-mast supporting the large antenna for the altitude-measuring radar (SP). Departing Norfolk on Sept. 5th, she sailed to Guantanamo Bay, Cuba for gunnery practice and sea trials. On the return trip to Norfolk, in a smooth sea, an eight-hour shakedown run was made during which she traveled at over 38 knots. After several days spent conducting tests on a new product to lay down smoke screens, Bordelon sailed for Casco Bay, Maine. As part of the Casco Bay Training Program, exercises were conducted off Nova Scotia and the crew was given training in extinguishing shipboard fires. The ship held an open house, in observance of Navy Day, in Portland.

In November 1945, Bordelon returned to Norfolk to prepare for a trip to Japan. The squadron arrived at Coca Sola, Canal Zone, on Nov. 11th and the next day transited the canal, en route to San Diego to load supplies. Three days later, with Dennis J. Buckley as flagship of Destroyer Div 16, the Bordelon, Leary and Dyess and the other Div. of destroyers were underway for Pearl Harbor, arriving on the 28th. After several days in Pearl Harbor, the eight destroyers continued toward Japan. On the way, a typhoon was encountered and the SP radar antenna had to be secured, as the rotation motors were unable to control the heavy antenna. At one point the Bordelon was rolled 54 degrees. Surviving the typhoon, they reached Yokosuka with less than a day's supply of fuel. After Christmas, the ships went to Kure, Japan for repairs from the tender, Vulcan. The storm had lifted the forward 5" gun mount of the Bordelon and the rotation gears had been crushed.

After repairs, the eight destroyers joined the Navy's first peacetime task force and then spent many days in training between Guam and Saipan. The first mission of Task Force 77 was to make an official call on the port of Hong Kong. Following a week in Hong Kong the ships went up the Yangtze River, into the Wangpoo River, to Shanghai for a week of liberty. In May 1946, the Bordelon, along with the Brinkley Bass DD 887, the Vesole DD 878, the Leary DD 879, the Dyess DD 880 and others, was engaged in maneuvers, torpedo runs, and tactical exercises. In late June the Task Force was sent to Manila to take part in Philippine Independence Day. In Dec. of 1946 Bordelon returned to the Atlantic Fleet, carrying over a hundred Navy and Marine veterans, as her home port was shifted to Newport, Rhode Island.

During April 1947 she was in Brooklyn Navy Yard. In the summer the ship made a Midshipman Cruise to Argentia, Newfoundland and Bar Harbor, Me. During the winter she made a northern European cruise, operating out of Plymouth, England for six months as part of the Northern European Task Force. The summer of 1948 saw another Midshipman Cruise to France, Portugal and Algeria. In 1949 she operated along the East Coast of the U.S. and then made her 1st Mediterranean Cruise.

In Sept., along with the USS Stribling, the USS Juneau and USS Columbia, the Bordelon entered the port at El Ferroll, Spain. This marked the first official visit by USN ships to Spain in over twenty years. In Nov. the Bordelon, with Vesole, Leary and Dyess, took part in a cold weather cruise as part of a task fleet in the North Atlantic, crossed the Arctic Circle and all hands received the Order of The Blue Nose. On May 3, 1950 the Bordelon left Norfolk for Lisbon, Portugal to again become part of the Sixth Fleet in the Mediterranean Sea. After various port visits and fleet exercises, Bordelon left Suda Bay, Crete on July 19, for Trieste, Italy. Transit of the Adriatic Sea was made at nine knots, in a narrow swept channel, due to the minefield remaining from WWII and, it was said, from WWI. On occasion mines, which had broken loose from their moorings, were observed floating on the surface. Upon being shot by the gunners, these mines usually sank rather than exploded. Bordelon arrived in Trieste on July 23 and stayed for ten days to support the Allied forces of the U.S. and Great Britain, who occupied the city, along with Russia. August 3rd through the 8th was spent in Venice, from which a quick return could be made to Trieste.

After more port visits and maneuvers, Bordelon sailed into Orinca Bay, Sardinia, on Sept. 22 to meet the relieving ships and depart the Sixth Fleet, headed for home. To celebrate the 4th of July 1951, Bordelon held open house in New Bedford, MA. During Aug and Sept., as part of DesRon 4, she hosted a group of ROTC Midshipman on their annual training cruise to Guantanamo Bay. Returning to the Mediterranean in Jan. 1952, Bordelon met the homeward bound ships in Gibralter. In March, after various port visits and exercises, including "Grand Slam" in Feb., the starboard propeller struck a submerged object, causing the shaft to vibrate. Bordelon entered an English dry dock in Malta, the propeller was replaced and the rudder was repaired. After a visit to Istanbul and then, Bari, Italy, Bordelon was one of the first American ships to make a post-war port visit to Yugoslavia.

Visiting Split in April, the officers and crew entertained a group from the embassy in Belgrade and the senior class of the Yugoslavian Naval Academy, as well as the children from the local orphanage. After visiting Trieste and Venice, she sailed to Gibralter to be relieved by the incoming ships and returned to Norfolk. In April 1953 Bordelon again went to the Med. In Oct., shortly before she was to return to the states, Bordelon hit a submerged log while backing to a refueling pier, in Caligliaria, Sardinia. This time there was extensive damage to the port propeller. A diver reported one blade with about 10 inches broken off and the tips of the other blades bent from 20 to 30 degrees. Bordelon limped to Gibralter at 8 knots for repairs at an English dry dock, and then sailed for home. In Dec. 1953 Bordelon served as one of two Presidential guard ships to cover the route of the president on the way to the Big Three Conference in Bermuda. In 1954, Bordelon entered the Navy Yard at Norfolk and the after the tripod mast was removed. A new height finding radar was installed with an antenna on an after-deck house. The 40 mm guns were replaced by 3" 50s. From 1956 through 1959 Bordelon was deployed with the Sixth Fleet in the Mediterranean three times and took part in two Northern European cruises. During this period Bordelon was awarded the coveted Battle Efficiency "E" and the ship's home port was shifted to Charleston, South Carolina. The 1958 cruise enabled the crew to visit the World's Fair in Brussels, Belgium.

The summer of 1959 saw the Bordelon evaluating new electronic gear which had been installed. From 1959 to 1963 Bordelon was again deployed with the Sixth Fleet in the Mediterranean, and participated in most of the Second Fleet and NATO air defense exercises that were conducted to develop new techniques of fleet anti-air warfare. In February 1962, the Bordelon participated in "Project Mercury" and the recovery of LTCOL John Glenn and his Mercury spacecraft from a US Manned Orbital Flight. Bordelon also participated in the Cuban Quarantine Operation. In Oct, Bordelon was positioned directly off Havana with the primary mission to alert Boca Chica if aircraft taking off from Havana airport did not make an immediate right turn after departing. Then the search radar at GTMO failed and Bordelon was ordered to proceed to GTMO at flank speed to serve as their back up air search radar system. The crisis ended while Bordelon was approaching GTMO.

In Feb.1963, Bordelon entered the Charleston Naval Yard to undergo a Navy program designed to extend the useful life of many of the ships constructed during WW II. As part of this Force Reconstruction and Modernization, (FRAM 1), the earlier bridge with the port holed inner wheelhouse was replaced with the roomier, single structure with full windows (with windshield wipers in front of the Captain's and OOD's chairs). This bridge added a lot of windage and slowed her down to approx. 27 knots, but in heavy seas the squadron FRAM II "Allen Sumner"'s, "James C Owens" (DD776) and "Strong" (DD758) would be forced to slow down to protect their older style bridge. Two ASW torpedo tubes replaced Mount 52 and the handling room became the forward officer's country. Bordelon received improved radar, sonar and communication gear. Amidships was mounted the ASROC launcher. Aft of the second stack was the ASROC magazine/DASH hanger. 4th Div bunked in the hanger bay. Above the hanger stood an ECM room with the array on a tower/mast. Sonar Control was moved from below the mess decks to port side behind CIC. The compartment below the mess decks was expanded and housed OC, OI and S Divisions. The sonar equipment (twice as much as in 1952) was moved to an air-conditioned compartment, port side of the compartment just forward of the mess decks, and one deck down. The starboard side housed the 3rd Div Sonar Techs and ASROC GMs. Bordelon was re-designated as a DD, and re-assigned to Desron Four.

Jan. 1965 saw her off to the Med. and the Red Sea. In July and August she was off the coast of Santo Domingo during the insurrection there. Oct. 1965 saw her in New York City for the World's Fair. In August 1966 she participated in the North Sea NATO Operation, "Straight Laced". After this operation, the ship visited Wilhelmshaven, Germany. The ship again deployed to the Mediterranean from Oct 1966 to Jan 1967. During Dec. 1966, she participated in the search and rescue operation for the victims of the stricken Greek ferry Heraklion. Bordelon put into the Charleston Naval Yard for overhaul in the spring of 1967.

Bordelon participated in the Vietnam conflict, as part of the US Seventh Fleet, while deployed to the Western Pacific from November 1967 to June 1968. The ship fired her first shots at an enemy, after twenty-two years of commissioned service, on 20 January 1968, while participating in Operation "Seadragon". In addition to Seadragon,

Bordelon saw action on the gun-line near the demilitarized zone, delivering 5,700 rounds of ammunition and the ship was credited with inflicting considerable damage upon the enemy, so much so, that she became known as "The Bloody B". Bordelon operated with carriers on Yankee Station, rescuing four aviators and participating in the rescue of another in the Tonkin Gulf, and rescuing a landing craft from hostile enemy waters. For her outstanding performance in combat on this deployment, the Bordelon was awarded the Meritorious Unit Commendation by the Secretary of the Navy. Citation: For meritorious service from 6 Dec 1967 through 12 May 1968 while deployed as a unit of the United States SEVENTH Fleet, in direct combat operations in support of free-world objectives in Southeast Asia. During this period, USS BORDELON demonstrated her superior ability while performing in Operation SEA DRAGON, naval gunfire support, "Yankee Station" Operations and various other combat assignments.

BORDELON's responsive, accurate, and voluminous counter battery fire during SEA DRAGON Operations contributed significantly to the success of each combat mission, in addition to preventing the enemy batteries from inflicting damage to herself and other SEA DRAGON units. In naval gunfire support, BORDELON delivered over 5,700 devastating rounds of ammunition in the face of hostile fire, attesting to the noteworthy unit excellence which has become her trademark. Continually operating well within range of enemy coastal defense sites to obtain optimum accuracy with minimum delay, BORDELON provided round-the-clock support for United States and Allied forces, thereby saving the lives of countless troops ashore. In addition, her exceptional performance was responsible for the rescue of five airmen in distress. The outstanding professional skills and dedication demonstrated by the officers and men of USS BORDELON while operating as a unit of the "YANKEE STATION" Aircraft Carrier Task Groups, were in keeping with the highest traditions of the United States Naval Service. All personnel attached to and serving on board USS BORDELON during the above-designated period, or any part thereof, are hereby authorized to wear the Meritorious Unit Commendation Ribbon.

After returning to Charleston, Bordelon participated in NATO operation "Silver Tower" off Norway. The ship visited Amsterdam upon completion of the exercise. In 1969 she again deployed to the Mediterranean, and in 1970 she was to be in the Middle East. Leaving Charleston in February, Bordelon crossed the equator and sailed around the Cape of Good Hope. Rounding the Cape, the ship was pounded by 40-ft seas, resulting in a 6-foot crack in the hull. This was repaired at the next port but the compartment that was flooded contained the ship's entire supply of toilet paper. Letters from home took on a new importance.

While in the mid-east, Bordelon was a back-up recovery vessel for Apollo 13, along with the USS Vesole. In 1971 she operated with several South American navies as part of UNITAS XII, visiting 6 South American countries and 17 ports, plus the Canal Zone and returning to Charleston to complete her 27th year of active service. In late January 1972, Bordelon deployed to Guantanamo, Cuba assigned to "Operation Johnny Express" She escorted freighters past Cuba for approximately 30 days. One evening, Bordelon received a distress call from the USS Beacon, PG99 which had collided with a small freighter, was on fire and flooding. Maneuvering in 12-14 foot seas, Bordelon put men and equipment aboard Beacon and kept her afloat. During this activity, Bordelon and Beacon collided and Bordelon sustained a 4 foot diameter hole in her port bow. Bordelon was able to tow Beacon until a fleet tug could take over and Bordelon returned to Gitmo for repairs and resumed her mission several days later.

Returning to the Western Pacific in Oct. 1972, Bordelon participated in Operation Linebacker, one of the heaviest naval actions in the Vietnam War. At one point, Bordelon lost her starboard turbine while shelling targets, leaving her exposed to shelling from the shore by 8" guns. With luck and cover fire from the USS Lawrence, Bordelon was able to withdraw with minimal damage. Bordelon went to Subic Bay to replace her turbine, fighting heavy typhoon seas while being able to make about 10 knots. After the cease-fire, she left the Seventh Fleet on 12 March 1973, after serving in the Western Pacific for 121 days, and arrived home in Charleston, SC on 5 April 1973.

CDR Carmody said the ship had steamed 40,000 miles and fired 4,000 rounds. The Bordelon participated in six strikes against the enemy and had a few thousand rounds fired at it by coastal defense forces. The ship also provided group support to forces in S. Vietnam and performed search and rescue duties on Yankee Station for aircraft. In July, although scheduled to return to the Med., the Bordelon was sent on a Central American tour as part of UNITAS XV. This included 5 days in Rio de Janeiro and a trip through the Straits of Magellan.

In April 1975, while re-fueling, the Bordelon collided with the USS Seattle AOE 3, resulting in only minor damage. Again in the Mediterranean in Oct. Bordelon completed anti-submarine operations in the Ionian Sea and rejoined the Task Force based on USS John F. Kennedy. During nighttime maneuvers in Nov., the Kennedy collided with the cruiser, USS Belknap CG 26. The USS Claude Ricketts, DDG 5, was ordered alongside upwind, to fight the midships fire on Belknap. When it was realized that little progress was being made with the fire, Bordelon was ordered alongside Belknap, downwind in the flame and smoke, to direct water on the area where no one else could reach. Cdr. George Pierce held Bordelon within fifteen feet of the side of Belknap -in open seas- until the fires were brought under control. Bordelon then towed Belknap to Augusta Bay, Sicily and aided the Belknap crew with repairs for three days. The holiday period was spent in Palermo, Sicily. During the summer of 1976, Bordelon participated in the USS Independence's ORI (Operational Readiness Inspection) and deployed to northern Europe as part of the largest maritime NATO exercise to date, "Teamwork 76".

On Sept 14th, while refueling alongside the USS John F. Kennedy, the ships came together and collided. The Bordelon's port bow and some of the superstructure were damaged and the main mast snapped and fell on the signal shack, injuring some of the handling team. Bordelon, escorted by USS Brumby FF 1044, sailed to the Devonport Royal Navy Yard in Plymouth, England. After 11 days getting repairs and a Pathfinder navigation radar, Bordelon, in company with the USS Kalamazoo AOR 6 and USS Luce DDG 38, proceeded under her own power to Charleston, SC. On Jan 6th, 1977 XO George Ellis relieved CDR George Pierce. Due to the damage to the superstructure and electronics and the age and condition of the hull, the Bordelon was decommissioned on Feb. 1, 1977. Cmdr. Pierce was cleared of blame during the post-collision inquiry and later commanded the USS Cone DD 866. Towed to Philadelphia by the USS Shakori ATF 162, the ex-Bordelon was stripped of usable equipment. Iran bought the remains, for boiler system parts, and had the hull towed to Iran. It was later sunk as a target. Bordelon was deployed 26 times and received 2 Meritorious Unit Commendations.

A history of the Bordelon - from the website

www.military.com Posted by Frank Doherty

Apr 05 2007 08:40:46:000PM

ABOUT THE AUTHOR

Terry Nardone was born in Rochester, NY. Home of the Eastman Kodak Company. Photography was all the rage, all the time.

He enlisted in the US Navy the day after his eighteenth birthday in 1971. He hoped to become a Photographer's Mate. The only school activity he participated in was Student Council.

He became heavily involved with the Vietnam Veterans of America and lobbied for veteran's issues extensively.

In 1993 he and his wife Michelle, along with his two sons, Corey and Chris moved to Hammondsport, NY. A small village on Keuka Lake in the Southern Tier of New York State.

CPSIA information can be obtained
at www.ICGtesting.com
Printed in the USA
BVHW041739161121
621784BV00011B/157